M000281097

The
BIRTH CALLED DEATH

The remarkable story of one woman's journey to the other side of life

KATHIE JORDAN

RiverWood Books
Ashland, Oregon

Copyright © 2003 by Kathie Jordan.

All rights reserved. No part of this book may be used or
reproduced in any manner whatsoever without written
permission except in the case of brief quotations
embodied in critical articles and reviews.
Inquiries should be addressed to:
RiverWood Books, PO Box 3400, Ashland, Oregon 97520.

www.riverwoodbooks.com

The author of this book does not dispense medical advice or prescribe the use of
any technique as a form of treatment for physical or medical problems without the
advice of a physician, either directly or indirectly. The intent of the author is only
to offer information of a general nature to help you in your quest for emotional
and spiritual well-bing. In the event you use any of the information in this book for
yourself, which is your consitutional right, the author and the publisher assume
no reponsibility for your actions.

Printed in the United States of America
First printing: 2003
Second printing: 2005

Cover design: David Ruppe, Impact Publications

Library of Congress Cataloging-in-Publication Data
Jordan, Kathie.
The birth called death / Kathie Jordan.--1st ed.
p. cm.
ISBN: 1-883991-77-3
1. Future life. 2. Spritualism. I. Title

BF1311.F8B57 2003
133.9'01'3--dc21
2003043109

The
BIRTH CALLED DEATH

Contents

This book is dedicated in loving memory of my mom,
Willie Mae Manning, my dad, Lee Manning Sr.,
and my brother, Troy William Swain.

I also would like to thank my brother, Lee Manning Jr.,
for being the best brother a "little one" could have; and lastly,
I would like to thank my husband, Jimmy, for his
encouragement, loyalty, support and love while I put
down on paper some of my childhood memories.

Love you all,
Kathie

1

A Child's Dilemma

"MOMMY, MOMMY, I SEE TROY." With these words, at the tender age of three, I announced to my mother that standing at the end of my bed was my brother who had recently died in the Korean War. Even at that age, I understood that the man standing in my room was somehow different from the man I had known in my short life. I remember my mother glancing toward the end of my bed and nodding once at her beloved son, declaring to me that she, too, could see him. It was a special moment that would mark the bond between the three of us: my mother, my brother, and myself.

I recall from those early days that not only could I see my brother, but I was able to see quite a number of beings, colors, lights, and vibrations around me and other people. Each time I mentioned such things to my mother, she would quietly agree. She never tried to discourage me because she was quite psychic and was very pleased that at an early age I was beginning to show evidence of being aware of things that were beyond the normal five senses. And yet she could not have guessed the degree to which I could see things. Being an intensely private person, I kept most of my observations to myself. But from time to time, comments would slip from me, which indicated to her that something extraordinary was taking place in our lives.

My father and brother, Lee, were normal in all of these respects, and regarded my mother and I with a fond tolerance. I suppose, in an earlier age, my mother and I would not have been so vocal in our pronouncements about dead people and future events. But, this was the fifties, and we were tolerated by those who knew about our secret world.

During my young life I was to see Troy many times. He would always advise me about various aspects of my life and would help me comfort our mother who continued to grieve for him.

I began to read at the age of four, and from that moment on, I read everything I could get my hands on. At that time, I also began to listen to the voices of the angels that I could see around me, and often times, I would dance and sing with the fairies who inhabited my back and front yards. What a strange creature my mother must have thought I was. But since she could see some of what I was seeing, I was left alone to pursue my visions.

At age seven, my life changed in a most dramatic way. One night while lying in bed I was feeling particularly happy with life, when once again I saw Troy.

He smiled at me very gently and asked, "Do you want to know what death is like?"

I looked at him and asked, "What do you mean? Am I going to die now?"

"No," he said, giving me a long, sweet look. "Now is the time to show you exactly what happens after death."

I smiled up at him and said, "Let's go!"

He held out his hand and I grabbed on to it, remarking in my mind how solid it felt.

He looked at me, as if he had heard the thought I just voiced in my mind, and said, "Look back."

As I did so, I could clearly see my body lying on my bed. A small but gentle smile was upon my face.

I asked him, "What would happen if my mother came into my room to check on me?"

"Your body would appear as if you were in a deep sleep."

I nodded, satisfied with his answer, then prepared myself to set off on this big adventure. I kept my eyes open because I wanted to experience everything. Since my religion at that time was Baptist I fully expected to go up. But in reality, my brother led me inward into another dimension.

The first thing I saw was a beautiful tunnel of light in which all the colors of the rainbow were reflected. As we passed through this tunnel, I saw other people walking along it.

I asked Troy, "Are all of these people dead?"

"Yes, they are. In fact, many of them have just died and are being guided along by close relatives who had died earlier."

I looked directly at the people and noticed that, although some of them looked confused, there was a beatific look on their faces; and in the glow of the colors I saw around them, an intense peace radiated.

As we neared the end of the tunnel, the welcome cries that greeted each person from those who had gone on before were so sweet that I made up my mind that after I had passed on to this realm, if at all possible, I would like to be there to greet my returning relatives and friends. As I passed several of these very happy reunions, some people who now inhabit these realms smiled and nodded at me.

As I acknowledged their smiles, I asked my brother, "Do these people normally smile at strangers as they pass through this tunnel?"

He actually laughed and said, "Of course! But someday, in the not-so-distant future, you will understand why you received those smiles."

I let that comment pass and allowed my brother to continue on with our journey. As we exited the tunnel, the first thing I saw was a very large valley surrounded by mountains. The valley was filled with a vast profusion of flowers and plants. All of the flowers were vibrating at a much higher rate; and from that vibration came the most melodious sounds I had ever heard. Even the colors of the flowers were brighter than any I had ever seen on Earth.

My brother answered my unspoken question. "Yes, Little One, what you are seeing are colors which vibrate at a much higher frequency, thus generating a different band of colors than those which you normally see on the Earth plane."

Little One. It was a phrase I would hear repeated often times in the future. I loved the sound of it.

As we journeyed deeper into the valley, I seemed to be floating. I asked Troy where we were going so many times that he finally asked me to be quiet.

After a while he said, "You will see soon enough."

Soon various dwellings began to appear.

"If this is death then why do people need to live in these dwellings?"

"Because this is only the beginning level. People use these dwellings to get acclimated to their new surroundings."

Immediately I noticed that no two dwellings were alike.

4

I commented on this and Troy responded, "Here people can use their imagination fully to create the type of dwelling they wish to occupy for the time being."

"Oh, kind of like drawing a house on paper; but here, the house is real."

"Very good. You learn quickly."

Inwardly I smiled. This was all so new and fascinating to me, that I wanted to go everywhere I could.

I asked Troy, "If this is only the beginning level then how many levels are there?"

"In the Bible, Jesus gave the answer to this question by saying, 'In my Father's house there are many mansions, if this were not so, I would not have told you.'"

Many mansions, I thought. How true! This verse in the Bible is one of my favorites.

I asked my brother, "How many mansions will I see?"

"Eventually, all of them. But this is true for everyone, in time."

I was completely enchanted by all that I was seeing. As my brother showed me around, what he called, one of the beginning levels of the afterlife, he could see how delighted I was by all of this. But I was also very curious about what people do here. I mean, after all, eternity is a very long time.

"Troy, what do people do here? Do they just sit around and play games? And by the way, where are their angel wings?"

My brother smiled at me good-naturedly. "No, sis. They spend a great deal of their time learning about the life they just left."

"What do you mean?"

"Well, it's very simple. Upon your arrival here, you spend some time resting. How much time, depends on the circumstances of your death. If you had a particularly violent death, then you may be allowed to sleep for some time."

"A few days?" I asked him innocently.

"No, more like a few months, or even a few years in Earth time. Remember, here there is no time or space. That is a concept that is restricted to the Earth plane."

I tried to imagine the condition of no time or space, even though, I was in that condition right then.

To help me understand this, Troy asked me, "How much time do you think has passed since you left your body to take this journey?"

I thought long and hard, and decided that at least a few hours had passed. So I said, "How about three hours, Troy?"

He laughed and said, "Actually, no time has passed since you left your body."

It would take me a few years to learn the truth of that simple statement. But at that point I just let it go.

I told Troy, "I simply do not understand."

"That's okay; someday you will."

"Getting back to your original question, once a person has rested, he is then reunited with one of his earthly guides, and together they review the life that has just ended. All aspects of the life are subject to a most thorough review. As one aspect of this review, the person is shown what he was expected to learn before he actually took birth. In other words, we as humans get a preview of our lives before we actually take birth. The purpose of this is to help us to remember the proper road to take for our growth at crucial times in our lives. We don't always do this successfully. But sometimes a faint memory is all the nudge we need to take the right fork in the road."

Troy assured me that the purpose of the life review is not to condemn, but to point out aspects that help us become better people and that help with our continuing evolution.

I asked Troy, "Does this review take place in the dwellings that each person creates for themselves?"

"Sometimes, but most of the time the review takes place in a special building created for that purpose."

"What does that building look like?"

"Like a movie cinema."

As we finished the conversation Troy said, "I can take you to more levels. Do you want to go?"

"Of course! But how do we get there?"

Troy then said something that astonished me to no end.

"Quite simply, my thoughts will take us to any level we desire to go to."

With that, we proceeded to go to many more levels. Each level vibrated at a higher rate and had even more subtle shadings of colors than I had seen on the Earth level.

All too soon my brother said the words I had been dreading to hear since the adventure began.

"Little One, I'm afraid it's time for me to return you to the Earth plane."

"No," I cried from the bottom of my soul. "I don't want to go back. Troy, please don't make me. I want to stay here with you forever."

He gave me a big hug. As we neared the mountain range that I had first seen upon my arrival to this beginning level—which I later learned is called the astral plane—he sat me down. As I turned to face him he spoke the words which I have never forgotten.

"Kathie, I know you want to stay here, but it is not yet

time. You have much to do on the Earth level before you will return to reside here."

"I don't care! This world is much more beautiful than anything I've seen on Earth. Please, Troy, don't make me go back."

"Now, honey, your mother has already lost one child, and it would hurt her too deeply to lose another one, especially a child who reminds her so much of the one she lost."

I knew that Troy was talking about himself, and how his death so deeply affected my mother. I also knew that, as much as I wanted to stay, I did not wish to cause my mother any more grief. I knew in my heart that Troy was right; I had to return.

With much reluctance, I turned my back on the beautiful mountain range and once again found myself in the tunnel of light. As I sped along the tunnel my heart seemed to get heavier and heavier.

Noticing this, Troy said to me, "I will come often to take you back to these levels, that you are leaving with such a heavy heart."

As we returned to my room on Earth, Troy showed me the proper way to reenter my body.

"You will know that you have gotten back into your body incorrectly if you 'wake up' and cannot move any part of your body. You will feel as if you have been frozen. Even breathing will seem difficult."

"What should I do in a case like that?"

"You should just go back to sleep. When you awaken, everything will be as it should be."

As I felt myself lowered into my body, I glanced at the face of my brother. He seemed well pleased with me. As he turned to go he said one last thing to me.

"Kathie, you will always remember this night. It is the start of a very remarkable journey."

"Okay, Troy," I murmured, sleepily. As I waved goodbye to him and fell into a deep and restful sleep, I wondered what he meant by his comment.

"Sleep well, Little One," I heard him say softly as he gradually faded away.

2

Just for the Fun of It

THE NEXT DAY WAS SATURDAY so I slept in a little late. When I awoke, I saw my mother hovering over my bed.

"What's wrong Momma?" I asked.

"Nothing. I had a hard time waking you up and I was getting worried."

"Oh, Momma, I saw Troy last night and he showed me what death is like."

My mother said nothing at first, then smiled slowly and said, "We will talk about it after breakfast. But right now, I want you to take a bath and get ready."

"But, Momma, I want to tell you what happened."

"I know you do, Kathie. But your bath water is getting cold, and besides, you can tell me all about Troy's visit later."

"Okay, but please don't let me forget to tell you. It was really a wonderful experience."

She looked at me, gave me a hug and said, "Scoot along."

Later on, after my bath and a good breakfast, I sat down with my mother and proceeded to relate to her my experience with Troy. As I told her about my journey, my mother would ocassionally nod her head in agreement.

"Have you ever had an experience like this one?"

"Yes, I was about fifteen years-old, and my own mother had passed away a year earlier. One night, she came to me and took me with her. I remember seeing a large tunnel of light and a very beautiful mountain range."

I got very excited as my mom was telling me her story. It coincided completely with what I had just experienced.

My mom then said, "I was only able to visit the first level."

"Why?"

"I don't know why."

I almost felt guilty because I had visited so many levels with Troy.

Not wanting to cause her any discomfort, because of having only seen the first level, I asked, "Did your mom come to see you more than once?"

"No, I only saw her the one time."

Inside, I felt a little worried. Would Troy only come to see me one time? But, no, he had assured me that he would come back to visit me many times.

"How did you like the other side?" Mom asked me.

"I loved it, and I even asked Troy if I could stay there."

She became very quiet and asked me, "Do you truly understand what you asked of him?"

"Yes, Mommy, I did not want to come back to Earth. So, I guess that would have meant that my body would have died."

I then told her what Troy had said.

I could see that his words touched her deeply because she began to cry, and then softly moaned, "I could not bear it if I lost you too. While I can understand and relate to the fact that you did not wish to come back, I am very happy that Troy had the wisdom and the courage to make you return to Earth."

She made me promise that, while she was residing on Earth, I would always return from my nightly sojourns.

As I looked into her beautiful face, I said, "I will always return to you. I will never allow myself to be swayed into staying on the other levels."

Crying, she gave me a very big hug and sent me to my room to begin my daily chores. As I turned to wave goodbye to her, I could see that my brother's words were indeed true. She could not have stood the death of another child.

Later that day, after I had finished my chores, I sat reading in my room and again heard my brother's voice.

"Hi Troy," I replied.

He sat down next to me and said, "Now, aren't you happy I made you come back?"

"Yes, Troy, you were right!"

I gave a big sigh and noticed him slipping away with the words, "I'll be back soon."

My mom came into the room just as Troy was leaving.

"Lunch time," she announced.

Hmm, I thought, after lunch comes a nap. What a good time for an experiment.

With that thought in mind, I followed my mother into the kitchen. My dad and brother were already there. I didn't think that my mom would mention my experience to them, and I was right. She knew that my dad was rather spooked by these type of experiences.

As I ate my lunch, I once again thought about my experience from the previous night. My mother gave me many meaningful glances because I was so lost in thought that I was unusually quiet. My brother tried to tease me out of my quiet state, but I just told him to leave me alone.

Even my dad noticed my silence and asked my mom, "Is there anything wrong with her?"

She glanced my way and I replied, "No, I'm just thinking about things."

After lunch, my mom sent my brother and I to our room to take our naps.

As I climbed into bed my mom whispered to me, "Please come back to me."

"I don't think I will see Troy again for a little while."

She smiled and said, "Okay, have a good nap."

As I closed my eyes, I thought about the little experiment that I wanted to try. I thought about what little I knew about death, and I tried to imagine that I was about to take my last breath. Would there be pain? Would my feet get cold? Would I feel the warmth slipping out of my body, from my feet up?

I tried to lie as still as possible. As my body became motionless, I remembered the tunnel of light. The more I thought about the tunnel, the lighter my body became. All of a sudden, there was a subtle pulsation and I felt myself begin to rise. I opened my eyes to see if it was my imagination and saw my body lying on the bed. A long silver cord connected my body to the self that was rising away from it. When I turned to look at the tunnel, I was filled with great excitement and joy. I had done it! I had gotten out of my body. This, to me, was what death must be like.

As I turned to go into the tunnel I saw Troy, who seemed a little perturbed.

"Kathie, you must not do this yet."

"Why not?"

"Because, you haven't learned the proper way to get out of your body, or to return to it once you wish to come back. You could experience all kinds of trouble if you are not careful. Especially at your young age."

"You mean the age of my body, right?"

Troy sighed, "Yes, little sister, I mean the age of your body. There is a time and a place for everything."

"Troy, does this mean that someday you will teach me more about getting out of my body and journeying to the levels beyond death?"

"Yes, Little One, but not today. Come now, let us return you to your body."

"Okay," I said, very reluctantly, "but you must come back soon. I want to learn everything I can."

He looked at me wisely and said, "I can tell that you will indeed fulfill your destiny."

"What do you mean?" I asked.

He laughed and said, "I am going to put off this discussion for another time."

"Okay," I replied as he gently guided me back into my body for what would prove to be a very long and restful nap.

After my nap, all I could think about were the events that had happened to me the previous night and that afternoon. My mother kept a very close watch on me for the rest of the evening. She seemed very concerned that I might forget my promise to her and remain on the other side.

Later that evening, as she tucked me into bed, I once again reminded her that I intended to keep my promise and would not try to stay on the other side. Satisfied with my comment, she said goodnight and I immediately fell into a deep and uneventful sleep.

As I dressed for Sunday School the next day I wondered when I would see Troy again. I hoped it would be soon.

At Sunday School, I asked my teacher many questions about what happens after we die.

My teacher asked me, "Why are you so concerned about death? Do you have a relative who is dying?"

"No, I'm just curious."

The teacher then said, "Basically, there are two places one can go to after death—Heaven or Hell."

"What exactly is Heaven? Is it a place where you fly around as an angel and sing songs to God? Do you do this for all of eternity?" I asked.

"Why, yes. That is the reward you receive for living a sin-free life here on Earth."

"But how can you live a sin-free life here on Earth if all about you is what seems like only trial and tribulation?"

"Well, this is where the good Lord Jesus Christ intervenes, and saves us from our sins. All we have to do is to believe in him and try to live a good and decent life."

"Oh, then all of those songs about the blood of the lamb are actually about the sacrifice of Jesus; that sacrifice being, his life for our sins."

"Yes, you are really understanding this well for someone so young."

I thought, boy does she have this wrong!

"What about Hell?" I asked.

"Well, I really don't want to scare you with fire and brimstone, but Hell is the place for unrepentant sinners."

"What's an unrepentant sinner?"

"Someone who lives his or her life in such a way as to

reject the gift that Jesus has to offer, and follows the evil side. For such a person, Satan is his master and Hell is the place where that lost soul will burn in fire for all of eternity."

"All of eternity?" I asked incredulously. "Boy, that is a very long time." I made a mental note to ask Troy about this the next time I saw him.

My teacher then asked me, "Do you now have a clearer understanding about death?"

"Oh, yes."

I wanted to ask her more questions, like what about people, in other lands, who have not heard the good news about Jesus, but lived a decent life? Would they be condemned to an eternity of fire just because they were ignorant of the true Savior? But I knew that I had asked enough questions for one morning.

As my teacher began the lessons for that day, I sat and pondered the meaning of her words. How could there only be a Heaven and a Hell since Jesus had said, "In my Father's house there are many mansions?" I knew that eventually I would ask my teacher this point. But at this time, I preferred to remain quiet.

At my Baptist church, Sunday school lasted for about one -and-one-half hours. Then, we were allowed to join the adults in the regular church service, where I often saw people from the other side enjoying the service also.

Later that afternoon I asked my father about Heaven and Hell, and he explained it to me in much the same way as my Sunday school teacher had. He also described how each human being has a soul that departs the body at the time of death. Then, depending on what type of life that soul led on Earth and God's judgment of that life, the soul would either go to Heaven or Hell.

"That sounds pretty strong," I told my father.

I made up my mind, then and there, that I was going to try to lead a good life. I certainly did not wish to go to Hell.

After dinner, I spent some time trying to read the Bible for clues about death, Heaven, and Hell. Soon it was time to go to bed.

Once again, as my mother tucked me into bed, she reminded me about my promise and asked me, "Have you seen Troy today?"

"No," I replied.

My mother gave me a kiss. I said my nightly prayers and soon was fast asleep. She need not have worried for I was not to see Troy again for six months. When I did, he had some answers for me regarding Heaven and Hell.

3

Remains to be Seen

"HI TROY. WHERE HAVE YOU BEEN?" I asked.

My brother looked at me with great joy. I was very happy to see him again. It had been six long months since I saw him last, and I had so many questions I wanted to ask him. But most of all, I wanted him to take me back, through the tunnel of light, to the delightful land that I saw on my previous journey.

I had been unable to get out of my body since my last encounter with Troy, and that had been a major source of disappointment to me. I suspected that my dear, departed brother had a little something to do with my being unable to escape my body.

As I gazed at him, he nodded his head in quiet assent. I was both angry and delighted to see him again. Angry, because he had made me wait so long, and delighted because maybe now he was going to take me back to what I call "the other side."

"How is Mother doing?" he asked.

"She is fine, and is no longer keeping a close watch on me. Apparently, I have finally convinced her that I am not going to leave Earth any time soon."

"Good," he nodded. "I don't want Mom to be worried that I am going to steal you away from her."

As I sat on my bed watching Troy, I couldn't quite believe that he had actually returned to me.

"Troy, would you tell me a little bit about dying? What does it feel like? Were you afraid?"

"I would love to answer your questions. But I prefer to take you back to the other side of life so that I can show you as well as tell you."

"Let's go now," I said.

Troy laughed and said, "I will return later in the evening so it will appear as if you are asleep."

I was a little disappointed that we were not going to go right at that moment. But I assured him that I could wait.

"Okay, Little One, until tonight."

With these softly spoken words, Troy disappeared. Wow, I thought, I'm going back to that incredible land tonight.

Bedtime seemed like such a long way away. I mean, I hadn't even had dinner yet.

"Kathie," I heard my mother call, "dinner will be ready in about an hour. Please come into the kitchen and help me."

"Okay Mom," I answered, a bit too gleefully. The sooner dinner was finished the better.

Dinner seemed to last forever. My mother, sensing that I was a bit preoccupied, asked me, "Are you feeling okay?"

"Yes, I'm just a little tired."

She nodded her head in quiet agreement and I finished my dinner. As usual, I asked my mother if I could wash the dishes. She looked at me with amusement.

"One day," she laughed, "you will not want to do any dishes at all."

How true her words are now. But then, I could only laugh in disagreement.

"No, mommy," my childish words rang out, "I will always want to do the dishes."

She just looked at me and grinned, knowing that someday I would eat those words.

After I had happily done all the dinner dishes, I went into the living room to watch television. I didn't pay any attention to what was on the television because I was too busy thinking about my upcoming trip to the other side. Soon, bedtime was upon us, and Lee and I had our evening baths.

After we said our evening prayers, my mother kissed us goodnight and whispered into my ear, "Return to me."

I looked at her in surprise, but had long ago stopped wondering about how she knew things without anyone telling her. I just smiled and promised her that I would return tomorrow.

As soon as my mom left the room, Lee fell into a deep sleep and I once again heard Troy's voice.

"Are you ready to go?" he asked.

"Of course," I said, in my most grown-up voice.

He laughed and gently led me out of my body and into the tunnel of light. Once again I saw various people walking down the tunnel. Most of them were greeted by their loved ones as they approached the end of the tunnel.

As I looked ahead of me, I could see the beautiful mountain range. Both Troy and I seemed to float above the mountains. I looked down and saw what appeared to be a small village surrounded by white light. As Troy and I gently floated down to the village, I mentioned to him that this village did not seem familiar to me. He was unusually silent as we landed near a building that radiated the strongest white light I had ever seen. As I glanced at Troy, there seemed to be a slight aura of sadness about him.

"Troy, why are you sad?"

He looked at me with tears in his eyes and answered, "For your understanding, I am going to relive my own death process so that you will know what it felt like for me to die."

I could not believe that he would do this for me.

"Are we here in this village so that as you tell me your story the white light will help to take away some of the pain of your dying?"

He looked at me in astonishment.

"How can a child of your age have such an understanding of how these things work?"

I shrugged my shoulders. Even I did not understand how I knew things sometimes, only that I did.

Troy then said, "The building that we now stand in front of is actually a very large hall with lots of tiny rooms inside."

"Troy, is this hall used only for the retelling of death stories?"

"Yes, each room has a cinema-type screen on the wall so that the reality of the death seems only like a movie. That way, if the death had been a painful one, then no pain is associated with the retelling of the story."

As I looked around, I saw that several rooms were occupied. Troy led me into a room. The walls were covered with a light green covering. The furniture was also green and on one wall was a large screen. There was a bed in the center of the room. As I walked around the room, I noticed that the room was actually larger than it had appeared on the outside.

Troy motioned for me to sit down and be very quiet.

After I had taken my seat, two of the most beautiful people I had ever seen walked in. Troy whispered to me that they had been his spiritual guides while he was on Earth, and that they were here to help him relive his death.

They spoke in quiet whispers and nodded briefly in my direction. I tried very hard to hear what they were telling my brother. But I was only able to catch bits and pieces of their conversation, which made absolutely no sense to me. After Troy had conversed with his guides he came over to me and said that he was about to begin. He asked me not to be frightened by anything I might see on the big screen.

"The pain of this death has been over for many years," he said.

As I settled nervously upon my chair, Troy climbed into bed and began to slowly quiet down. I watched as he began to fall asleep, or so it appeared to me.

Without warning, I heard a loud noise on the screen and I nearly jumped out of my seat. As I gazed at the screen, I finally understood that this is war. It seemed as if the events on the screen had taken over my consciousness because that was all I could see. In my chair, I ducked as I heard bullets whining over my head. I saw other soldiers ducking also. Every once in a while I heard screams of pain as a bullet found its mark. I looked around and only saw other soldiers. I was in a foxhole. Where is the enemy, I wondered? Why are they shooting at me? What did I do to deserve being here in this awful hell?

Suddenly, I heard a soft voice questioning, "Is she really ready for the revelation she is about to receive?"

Another voice answered, "Let her experience it. She must understand the fear that people have about this final event."

Fear indeed was all around me. I smelled it and sensed it. The soldiers around me knew that they could die at any moment. Yet, they were brave boys, all willing to fight until the end if necessary. Seconds later someone shouted that a mortar was coming in and that everyone should take cover. I ducked down and felt the ground shake underneath me. Dirt seemed to be flying everywhere. The soldier next to me shouted, "That was a close one." We all stood up and began firing our weapons. Somewhere, in the back of my mind, was the thought that a seven-year old girl should not be in a foxhole, firing a weapon at some unknown and unseen enemy. Yet, somehow I knew it was right.

As I stopped to reload my weapon, I heard a strangled shout about another mortar coming in. Immediately I felt the most intense pain of my life. It seemed as if a portion of my body had exploded. I heard screaming, and soon realized that it was my own voice I was hearing. I opened my eyes and the world appeared to have gone red. The pain was everywhere and with everyone. I heard some moaning and looked over to my right to see a soldier with the bottom half of his body missing. He looked at me with a blank stare and quietly closed his eyes. I was unable to move and began to complain about how the cold was creeping up from my feet. I turned my head to the left and noticed that the whole upper left side of my body was gone. Shoulder, arm and hand, just gone. In that second, I knew I was dying. I closed my eyes, wondering how long it would take, noticing that the cold had reached my stomach.

At this point, the red mist seemed to clear and I saw two beings dressed in white. As I gazed upon their faces, the pain seemed to fade away. As the cold reached my chest area, I heard them beckoning me to leave. I watched as I gradually left my body behind. I looked around to see if this experience was happening to any of my other buddies, and I could see that indeed some of them were leaving their bodies. Others, who were not badly hurt, appeared to be sleeping. Just as I cleared my body, I felt a strong pull and realized that if I left my body behind, I could never return to it. Momma, I thought, you will be so devastated when you learn what has happened here, and how my life has ended.

My two guides helped me to understand that my mother's guides would help her during her time of need. Now I could feel the cold completely enveloping my body, and I watched as I took my last breath. As I did so, I suddenly felt very free. The pain was gone, although the memory of it was still very strong. As I turned to my guides, I discovered that I was in a tunnel of white light. I felt myself being pulled along the tunnel and did not fight what was happening to me. I quickly arrived at the end of the tunnel and was greeted by both my grandparents.

I heard my name called gently, "Kathie."

I turned and stared at my brother, who now seemed so whole and happy. I turned my head to my left, just to make sure that my seven-year old body was still intact. I now totally understood why my mother was unable to watch war movies, and I knew, from this moment forward I would be unable to view them. As I turned toward my brother, I heard his two guides tell him that it was very unusual for someone viewing the death scene of another to become so totally involved in it. It was as if I had become my brother in order to experience his death. Troy came to me and picked me up. He wanted to reassure himself that I was indeed none the worse for my experience.

"Troy," I said, "you do not need to say anymore. I understand completely."

As we left the hall I asked Troy if he had attended his own funeral. He told me that he had but only so that he could bring some measure of comfort to our mother.

"Do people often attend their own funeral?" I asked.

"Only if they are strong enough. Sometimes the shock of seeing your own dead body causes some people to try to return to it, even though they know that their life in that body has ended."

"What happens if someone attends their own funeral and tries to re-enter their body?"

"Well, most of the time that would be impossible because their guides would be there to help prevent it. But, if by some chance they did reenter their body, then they would either be pulled out immediately or be allowed to stay in it for a few hours. Usually, that is all that is needed to convince someone that their body has outworn its usefulness."

"Troy, was your funeral very bad?"

"No. Although mother was grief stricken and I wanted to be with her in the worst possible way, I knew that my time on Earth was done. Speaking of which, it is time for me to return you to the Earth plane."

"Troy, will you come and get me again soon?"

"Yes, I won't wait as long next time."

With that thought in mind, I returned to my body on Earth, and slept solidly through the night.

4

Glorious Times

"You're different," my mother said to me for what seemed to be the millionth time.

"Mom, I don't know what you're talking about? I'm the same old Kathie."

"No you're not. You seem quieter, and much more inward."

I let out a huge sigh. How could I tell her that I had experienced Troy's death? That I had actually died as him, not just once, but many times in my mind.

"Mom, how did Troy die?"

She gave me a sharp glance.

"Why do you want to know?"

"I'm just curious, that's all?"

She seemed to stare into space for a long time before she answered. I knew that it pained her to talk about it. But, I just had to know if what I had seen was really true or not.

"On the day that he died, I somehow knew that he was gone. Yet when I got the news, my heart stopped and a part of me died also." She turned and looked at me. "You're too young to fully understand. But I'll tell you this, he was hit in the left shoulder by a mortar shell, and was killed instantly."

"Are you sure that he didn't feel any pain?"

"I was told that he didn't experience any pain because his death happened so quickly."

I wished that I could tell her what had really happened. But I knew that it would not do her any good to know what I now know to be the truth. It was better for her to think that Troy's death was a quick and painless one.

I softly said to her, "I will not ask you any more questions about Troy's death."

Before the subject was closed for good, she mentioned that I had attended Troy's funeral. Try as I might, I couldn't remember the event. It was as if that portion of my life was much too painful for me to remember. Perhaps the sight of my mother's grief was too much for a two year-old to comprehend. I let the subject drop when I saw how sad my mother had become.

"Can I go outside and play?"

With that question, I dropped the subject of Troy's death, with her, forever.

Several hours later, as bedtime approached, my mother asked me, "Have you seen Troy lately?"

"Yes, I saw him last night."

She just nodded her head and quietly prepared my brother and me for bed. As I knelt down to say my nightly prayers, I asked that no more of my mom's children be taken away from her, for a long time to come. I was afraid of what any new grief would do to her.

As she tucked me into bed, she asked, "Would you express my love to Troy if you should see him tonight?"

"Yes, Momma, I will tell him, although I'm sure he already knows."

She smiled and kissed me goodnight.

As I began drifting into sleep, I felt a tug in the area of my navel. I looked up to see Troy floating over me.

"Let's go," he said. "I have many things to show you tonight."

I jumped out of my body and followed Troy through the tunnel of white light.

"Where are we going this time?" I asked, trying to keep up with him. He didn't reply to my question, so I kept quiet.

I wondered how is he able to go so fast. I just couldn't seem to keep up. As we reached the end of the tunnel, I once again saw the glorious valley. Troy turned to me and gently gathered me into his arms as we sped towards the center of the valley. Nestled in his arms, I was content to just let him take me wherever he wanted to go. Just as I was about to fall asleep, we arrived at a very large pink and white building.

"Kathie, this is a place where some come once they leave their bodies. I am being allowed to show you this place in order to help calm your fears about death and dying."

I nodded quietly and entered the building with my brother. The first thing I noticed was the quiet, except for some background music that was both soothing and exhilarating. As I watched, I saw many people entering the building, and being led to various rooms. Most appeared very stunned and looked around the building in a state of profound disbelief.

"Troy, what is going on here? Who are these people?"

Troy took me aside, and informed me that, except for myself, all of these people had just died. I turned around to glance at them once again. As I was watching, I saw a young woman come in. She was greeted by what I assumed to be her spiritual guide.

"Do you want to follow her, to see what happens?" asked Troy.

"Of course!"

"It's all right! But we must keep very quiet and not intrude upon her afterlife integration process."

As we followed the young woman, down a long hall-way, she seemed very subdued. Soon, a door to one of the rooms opened and all of us entered. The young woman then walked over to the bed, that was along one of the walls, and laid down. I heard her spiritual guide tell her to just let go and fall sleep.

The woman looked around her, saw me and asked, "Why is she in the room with me?"

My brother quickly went up to her and explained that I was still alive and was being shown what death is really like.

"You mean, I really am dead?" she exclaimed in a frantic voice.

"Yes," he replied. "But in actual fact, now you are really alive. The life you lived on Earth was only a small part of your eternal existence."

He could see that she didn't really understand what he was trying to tell her. But felt soothed by his loving and kind words.

"Sleep now," one of her guides said, "and when you awake, your understanding will be much greater."

She once again glanced at me and asked, "Can she lie down next to me, just until I fall asleep? She reminds me of the daughter that I just left behind on Earth."

"Is that okay?" I asked her guides.

"Yes, she will be asleep in a very short time," one of them said.

True to the guide's words, she did indeed fall asleep very quickly.

"Troy," I asked, "was her death very traumatic?"

"Yes, she was murdered by her husband who wanted to collect the insurance money from her estate."

"How awful! Will she be okay?"

"During her sleep we will heal her of the trauma of her death," one of her guides said.

"I hope eight hours of sleep will be enough to do the job," I said.

Troy laughed very heartily.

"What's so funny?" I asked.

"Kathie, you do not understand," said Troy. "She will be asleep for many years. Such was the trauma of the death inflicted upon her."

I looked at him in astonishment. Years, I kept repeating.

"How many years?"

"Well, depending on the depth of the psychic damage, it could be anywhere from one to one hundred years."

"How could anyone sleep for a hundred years?" I asked him in utter disbelief.

He just smiled and said, "Easy! They sleep for as long as is needed and they usually awaken by themselves when they are ready."

"Is their sleep similar to the type of sleeping they did while on Earth?"

"Yes and no. They do dream a little bit. But while they are sleeping, their guides and, more importantly, the beings who have dedicated a portion of their existence to working with the people in this building, help them to understand what happened to them during their last moments on Earth, and the joys that now await them upon their awakening into this new life."

"Do all people come here after death? I mean, do all people come to this building to sleep after they leave their bodies behind on Earth?"

"No, not everyone comes here. People whose deaths are more natural usually do not need to come here. Or, if they do, they only sleep for a very short time."

As I slowly got out of bed, so as not to disturb the young woman, I realized that I didn't even know her name.

Aware of my unspoken thought, Troy replied, "That doesn't matter. What does matter is that you were able to give her some comfort."

As I left her room, I was assured that we would some-day meet again. She now seemed so peaceful lying upon her bed. Her guides had already surrounded her with the softest, pinkest light I had ever seen. I knew that she was going to be okay.

"Do you want to see some people as they awaken from their sleep?" asked Troy.

"Yes," I replied.

He began leading me into another part of the building. We seemed to float up some stairs until I stood in front of a row of beds. They were all evenly spaced, as if they had once been separated by walls.

"Very good," I heard Troy say. "People who are about to awaken from their sleep are grouped together by having their beds transported into this area. We find that waking up in a crowd seems to help."

As I watched with great interest, I noticed several people beginning to awaken. They all seemed quite content and refreshed. As each one sat up, his or her guide softly spoke to them, asking them if they were ready to continue their journey. They all nodded yes and quietly put their hands into the hands of each of their respective guides.

As their guides began to lead them away, I asked Troy, "Where are they going?"

"Each one of them has a temporary dwelling place that has been prepared for them, based on the types of places they enjoyed while living on Earth. They are now going to reside in these 'homes' for a short time."

"Troy, do you have such a home here?"

"Actually, my home is on another level. But I have taken the opportunity to have one constructed on this level so you can stay there when you journey to this life."

"Can we go there now?"

"Of course!"

As Troy led me out of the building, I noticed many people leaving the building on their way to their new lives. As we glided by numerous dwellings, I began to notice the various homes in different areas. It all seemed like such a crazy patchwork of designs and styles.

Troy answered my unspoken question, "Yes, Little One, you can have any type of house you want."

Soon we arrived in front of a very simple white house.

"This is home," Troy announced.

Upon entering, I noticed that everything about his house was very simple. The furnishings were both elegant and comfortable.

"Troy," I asked settling down on his sofa, "what do people do here? I mean, do they eat meals, do they play games? What is the meaning of all this?"

"Now, that is a question that has plagued mankind for

eons. Here you learn the answers to all of your questions. You don't go through life only to die, come here, build a house, and have things go on as if you were still on Earth. Here, we have schools and teachers to help us understand the meaning of our lives."

"You mean, you have to go to school here?" I couldn't help but ask that question. "You live on Earth, you go to school. You die and come here, and still you go to school. That's not very appetizing to me at seven years old."

Troy laughed and said, "Let me take you to the Hall of Records. That will help you gain a small measure of understanding."

"What is the Hall of Records?"

"Come, let me take you there."

Once again, as I traveled along with my brother, I couldn't help but marvel at the profusion of colors and heavenly sounds. Soon we arrived at a very large building that seemed impossibly high to me. As we went inside, I noticed that there were many people. Some of them seemed happy and content, but most seemed sad.

"Troy, why are these people sad? What have they seen that has caused them such sadness?"

"Come. Let's go into one of the many rooms and I will show you why."

We came to a door that seemed to suit Troy's purpose and we went inside. The room was colored in the most subtle of pastel colors, which I soon noticed began to change from one color to the next. The room had a large screen on one wall and a very comfortable sofa in the middle. As we sat down the lights dimmed, just as though we were in a movie theater, and the screen came to life. I was very surprised to see myself on the screen. I was looking at a scene from the previous day.

"You are," said Troy, reading my thoughts.

I saw everything I had done in the last twenty-four hours. I mean everything. Nothing was hidden. I could even hear what I had been thinking.

"Troy, how far back can this screen go?"

"As far back as is needed, to remind the viewer of exactly what took place in their life. Usually this starts from the moment of birth and continues on until the person dies."

How embarrassing, I thought.

"Does anyone see this other than the person whose life is the main focus?"

"Yes. Usually when someone is in this building to review their life, their guardian angels are there to help them through the sadness of seeing all their missed opportunities. You would not believe how rough people can be on themselves. They have to be watched very carefully when reviewing their life, to keep them from having too many harsh judgments of themselves. Usually, people have to come here many times before they can objectively view their previous life and begin learning some of the lessons they were meant to learn during their lifetime."

"Is it called the Hall of Records because every moment of your life is recorded, and if you wish, played back for your review?"

"Not, just if you wish, Little One. Before anyone can advance from this level they must have some understanding of the life just ended, and the many lessons they were supposed to have learned. Some were learned and some were not. That is where the sadness comes from: in seeing all of the lessons that were not learned and in having lived a life that was not lived up to its fullest potential."

"I now understand."

I was feeling sad about some of the things that I had done in the last twenty-four hours and made up my mind that I would try to live a better life.

Troy smiled.

"Troy, can we return to your house on this level. I have so many more questions to ask you."

"Little One, it is almost dawn on the Earth level and you must return now. There will be plenty of time to answer all your questions."

I knew he was right, and returned to my body, to face a new day in my life.

The next morning I asked my mother, "What would you do if you could review your life while still here on Earth?"

"What do you mean?"

"I mean, if somehow you could look back on the last twenty-four hours of your life, with a magnifying glass, and try to see what you could learn from it."

"Oh, you mean, if I could go and look at the Akashic Records."

"The Akashic what?"

"The Akashic Records. A place where you can go to see anything and everything that has happened previously on Earth."

"Mom, how do you know about this, and why do you call it the Akashic Records?"

My mother smiled at me, in a secretive way and asked, "Do you think you're the only one who can get out of your body and travel around?"

She knew that I wanted to ask her a million questions. But at that moment my father came into the room and I knew that this conversation would have to wait.

Later that evening my mother informed me that at times

she could look into the Akashic Records for whatever information she needed.

"How do you do it?" I asked her.

She shrugged her shoulders and said, "Even I am not sure how I do it. I just focus my attention in that direction and can see into the records. Perhaps some day you will understand how I do this."

"That's okay mom. If I need to know, I'm sure the information will come to me."

She smiled at me and announced that it would soon be bedtime. I didn't know if I would see Troy this night. But if I didn't, I knew that there would soon be other nights. As I drifted into sleep I thought about all that I had learned from my brother. It certainly helped me to understand life a little bit more. If only more people could find out about the wonderful life that exists after death. If so, people may be less fearful about the end of their earthly existence. With this thought in mind, I fell asleep.

5

School Days

ANOTHER SIX MONTHS PASSED before I saw Troy again. During that time, I tried to understand all that I had seen. I also asked my other Sunday school teachers about death and their answers were always filled with descriptions of Heaven and Hell. Certainly not anything I had seen as yet.

Of course, they wondered about this eight year-old child who was asking such detailed questions about life and death. During that time, my devotion to God grew a hundredfold. I constantly prayed to God for understanding of what I had seen and heard during my visits to the afterlife.

It was during one of my intense prayer sessions that I heard the now familiar voice of my brother.

"Kathie," I heard him call, "it's time for school."

Somehow, that did not ring true to me. After all it was early evening and unless I had fallen asleep, it was not time to get up and go to school.

"Yes it is!" exclaimed Troy.

With that comment, he pulled me out of my body. Once again, I found myself in the tunnel of light. This time it was full of people.

"What happened, Troy? Why is it so crowded?"

"There has been a natural disaster and many people have died."

"Are they going to be okay?"

"Yes. They're dazed and confused but many guides are waiting for them at the end of this tunnel. They will help them adjust."

I had almost forgotten.

"What school are we going to?" I asked.

"The first school most people go to when they are ready."

"Troy, is this a real school?"

"Of course, with real teachers and real school hours."

"Why would people want to go to school when they have just graduated from the biggest school of them all?" I asked.

Troy laughed.

"How right you are, Little One, about Earth being the biggest school of them all. The purpose of going to school on the various levels of the other side of life is to refine the lessons learned while on Earth, and to continue growing."

"For what purpose? Please don't tell me that I have to wait for the answer?"

"My, my, how impatient you have become! You are like a dry sponge waiting to soak up as much water as you can."

I had to laugh. His description was so accurate.

"That's okay, Troy. I'll wait until we get to the classroom and then I'll ask as many questions as I want to."

He smiled at me, and said very softly, "I truly doubt

that you will be asking very many questions."

As we arrived at a very beautiful yellow-hued building, Troy and I stepped inside and were directed to a very large room, complete with desks, books, and all of the usual items one sees in a schoolroom.

Troy asked me, "Where do you want to sit?"

"Anywhere, it doesn't matter. As long as we don't sit right up front or in the last row in the back."

So we sat down in the middle. As I glanced around the room, I saw people of all ages, sizes, and colors. Just as I was about to ask Troy a question, the most beautiful person I had ever seen walked into the room. The light around his body was filled with many pastel colors. Everyone in the room sat up at once as this person entered the classroom.

He nodded at Troy and said, "My name is Ariel and it is my job to help you understand what has just happened to you, and to help you make the necessary adjustment from earthly life to what we call astral life. I will only take questions at the end of the class because only then will you have enough knowledge to ask pertinent questions."

I started to ask Troy what pertinent meant and Troy whispered to me, "Not now. Just wait, and before too long you will understand."

Ariel began by saying, "First of all, understand that your earthly life is indeed over. You are now on the plane closest to Earth, called the astral plane. There are many levels of existence and in many respects this is the beginning level. As some of you are aware, there are several levels of the astral plane. However, you are not on the lowest astral level. That level is reserved for what we call our hard-core cases: people whose earthly existence left much to be desired. Some of you may call this lower level "Hell," and to those who exist there, that is a very apt description. People do eventually leave that level but it normally takes many years of rehabilitation. However the subject of this lowest astral level will be dealt with in other classes.

The astral level that you are currently on is considered a beginning level. It is for people whose lives on Earth were basically good. We try to maintain this level as similar to Earth as possible so you will be comfortable during your stay here. How long you stay is dependent on how quickly you understand what we are teaching you.

Here, all of you have homes that have been provided to you. Later, I will teach you how to change your homes so they reflect your own tastes and needs.

Also, we have surrounded you with loved ones, as guides to help you adjust. These loved ones have voluntarily descended from their own levels to be with you and to watch over your growth.

As some of you have noticed, there is day and night here. There are stores and places to eat so that you will feel at home here, as much as possible.

The one thing we would like you to do is not to worry about the speed of your progress. After all, you do have all the time you need."

Some people laughed a little nervously.

"Also, from time to time, as you grow and learn, there will be other teachers who will periodically teach this class. Graduation occurs when you have understood all there is to know on this level. There will be no group graduation because all of you will be allowed to grow and learn at your own pace. Some of you will notice, after a time, that people will start to disappear out of this class. Please, do not be alarmed if it turns out that you are one of the last ones left.

As I have indicated before, this class is more of an individual effort than a group one.

Also, some of you may have noticed that we have a visitor to this class; a young lady who still resides on the Earth plane. She will be visiting this class from time to time because of what she needs to learn while still on Earth. It is not very often that people living on Earth are able to visit this realm and remember what they have seen. But when we find such a person, they are always welcome to sit in on any classes that are needed for their growth. You may wonder how I know that she still resides on Earth. Well, I will show you. Kathie, could you please stand up."

As far as I was concerned, this was the worst thing that could have happened. I didn't want to stand up in front of all of these people. But at the urging of Troy, I did so.

Ariel asked, "Does anyone notice anything unusual about Kathie?"

Everyone turned to look at me. But no one seemed to notice anything strange. So Ariel pointed out the cord that was attached at my navel and stretched off into the distance.

"That cord is keeping her attached to her body on Earth. If all of you look at your own bodies you will not see a cord. Also, please notice that her cord itself is alive. See how it pulsates and is constantly changing color. At the time of death the cord is cut and you are then free to leave your body forever. Once the cord is cut, you cannot return."

As I glanced around the room, I noticed that not one person in the room had even a hint of a cord. Ariel indicated that I could now sit down and I did so with an audible sigh of relief.

"To people on Earth, death seems like an ending rather

than a beginning. I'm sure that many of you would like to visit the relatives and friends that you left behind on Earth, to let them know that you are alive and well. However, in the beginning this is rarely permitted. The people who are left behind on Earth must learn to adjust to their loss and continue on with their lives. You, who have recently arrived on this level, are beginning a new adventure; one that will require all of your concentration and understanding. When you do visit your relatives and friends it will take place in their dream state. It is during this time that they can, and often do, leave their bodies and visit on this astral level. These visits usually bring a measure of comfort to relatives and friends because they know that sometime in the future they will see their loved ones again."

A gentleman by the name of Tom smiled broadly.

"Do you want to say something?" Ariel asked him.

"Yes. I saw my wife in my dreams many times after she died. At first I thought I was having these dreams because of my intense grief. Later I was comforted when I awoke in the morning and knew that my beloved wife had been with me while I was asleep."

I then understood why my mother seemed so much more relaxed in the morning. She had often told me about her dreams of Troy. I glanced over at Troy who smiled at me and nodded his head in quiet assent.

Ariel then said, "If anyone has any questions, I would be glad to answer them."

No one spoke up at first. They all seemed so lost in their thoughts.

Finally, Tom asked, "Will I be permitted to see my wife, Emily, more often?"

"Emily has been away from the Earth level for close to

fifty years. She has already taken these beginning classes and resides on one of the upper levels, above and beyond the astral level. However, your life on Earth was a good one and you will most likely be with your beloved Emily soon."

Tom nodded his head and smiled. That was all he needed to hear.

The other people in the class had no questions, and I was too shy to ask. I felt like I was an intruder, although Troy was quick to assure me that I was not.

Since no one had any additional questions, Ariel ended the class, saying that the next time we met, he would discuss exactly what happens at the moment we are separated from our bodies.

As people filed out of the room Troy asked me, "Do you want to meet Ariel?"

"Oh, no, I'm sure that Ariel is too busy to speak with me."

Indeed, a small group of people had gathered around him. Troy indicated to me that my reticence was pure nonsense and that I should meet Ariel straightaway. As we walked up to Ariel the people that had gathered around him turned to look at us. Ariel smiled as I walked up to him.

He looked straight into my eyes and said, "No introductions are necessary, Troy. I know exactly who she is and I welcome Little One to my class."

I held out my hand for him to shake it and instead he kissed it.

"Little One, please know that you are always welcome to attend any of my classes that you desire."

"Thank you. I would like to come as often as I can."

Troy beamed down at me and indicated to Ariel that he would bring me as often as he could. At that moment, I noticed what appeared to be a silent communication between them.

Troy nodded his head and said to Ariel, "Yes, I know."

Ariel then replied, "Try to bring her here often. I want to be around her as much as I can, before you take her to the higher levels."

"Don't worry," Troy laughed. "You'll see her so much, I'm afraid you'll soon tire of her."

"Never, and that's a promise."

As Troy and I turned to leave the classroom, I could hardly wait to ask him what that little exchange had been about.

But before I could do so he said to me, "You will get your answers, all in good time. Now it is time for me to return you to your body."

As we traveled through the tunnel of light, I again noticed a great rush of people going the other way. Some were actually dancing through the tunnel. How odd, I thought. I guess they were happy to be out of their bodies. Troy then mentioned to me that the people I had witnessed, dancing through the tunnel, were much older people and happy to be free of their old and weakened bodies. Also, those people had relatives and friends waiting to welcome them.

Soon I arrived at my earthly home. As I was rejoining my body, I heard Troy say, "I will come and get you later."

"Okay, Troy," I murmured, as I settled into my body. I heard my mother calling me, letting me know that dinner was almost ready.

As I stood up to go into the kitchen, I smiled very happily. I knew that I would probably not see Troy later this evening. But that was okay with me.

The next morning, the events of the previous late afternoon were so strong in my mind that I wrote down what had happened in the journal that I was keeping.

When I saw my mother, I asked her, "Do you have very many dreams of Troy?"

"Not as many as I used to."

"Your dreams are real, Mom."

"I know. It is good that I can at least see him from time to time at night."

A few days later, just as I was drifting off to sleep, I heard Troy's voice and felt a tug in my naval area.

As I felt myself drifting higher and higher I heard Troy say, "Let's go sleepyhead, Ariel is waiting."

I hurried along at the mention of Ariel's name. After all, this was the second class and I didn't want to be late.

Troy grabbed my hand and literally carried me along the tunnel of light until once again we stood in front of the huge yellow-hued building. As we entered, Troy said to me, "I want you to pay special attention to the subject of this class."

"Okay, Troy."

Once again, we entered the classroom and took our seats in the middle. As far as I could tell, the class had all of the same people I had seen on my previous visit.

There was a slight murmuring in the classroom as Ariel came into the room. He was dressed in the most beautiful purple robe I had ever seen. The color almost seemed alive, it was so brilliant and vibrant.

Ariel began the class with a silent nod of his head to everyone in the room. The atmosphere was one of expectation and wonderment.

Ariel then began to speak, "How many of you died a violent death?"

Silence.

It seemed as if Ariel had asked the most uncomfortable question he could have asked. At first no one replied. Then, from the corner of the room came a very small voice.

"I did," a woman said.

Ariel turned to glance in that direction and indicated that the owner of the voice should stand up. All eyes turned in her direction as she stood up.

The compassion in Ariel's eyes was so intense that it felt to me like he was trying to ease her pain. Although the woman seemed very nervous, her voice was full of confidence.

"My name is, or rather was, Muriel. I'm twenty years-old and my husband thinks that he killed me," the young woman said.

Muriel hesitated for a moment, and Ariel indicated that she should go on. She took a deep breath and began her story.

"My husband and I had been married for a year. It was the most wonderful time of my life. But, the joy of that first year was nothing compared to the moment when the doctor told me that I was going to have a baby. I knew that when I told my husband, our joy would be complete.

After I had driven home, I planned how I would tell him. I wanted it to be a special moment, you see. He phoned to tell me that he was going to be a little late and not to make dinner, as he had a surprise for me. I waited for him to come home. When he did so, he explained that he had gotten a promotion and wanted to take me out to dinner, and afterwards, take a romantic drive along the coastline. I thought that that would be perfect; I could tell him about the baby after dinner.

We went out to dinner and when I told him I was pregnant, he was so happy he began cry. As we drove home, we were so full of plans and dreams. You have to understand, my husband was a very careful driver — even more so when he found out that I was pregnant. But, I guess nothing can prepare one for a wrong-way driver.

"I remember my husband telling me that he was concerned about the oncoming driver. As I looked out the front window, I noticed the car that he was talking about, but it seemed a great distance away. We were still talking when I heard my husband yell for the foolish driver to look out. As I looked up, the car seemed headed directly for us."

At this point, Muriel held her head down and began to cry very softly.

Ariel asked Muriel, "Do you want to go on?"

"Yes," she replied.

She then began to finish telling us her story.

"As the car headed straight for our car, my husband slammed on the brakes and simultaneously yelled, 'No, no.' At this point, everything seemed to slow down. I heard the crunch of the two cars meeting. Then I felt the most horrendous pain I have ever experienced. I will always remember the look on my husband's face. I heard him crying my name, over and over again. Then everything faded to black.

I could hear my husband call my name, as if from a great distance. He seemed to be screaming repeatedly 'Muriel come back, please come back to me.' Once again, I felt the agonizing pain of my body and tried to focus my eyes on my husband's face. He had been crying. 'Muriel,' I heard him say, 'please don't go. I can't live without you.' As I gazed into his eyes, I told him how much I loved him and that I would some day come back to get him. You see, almost every bone in my body had been broken; because I had been thrown from the car and had struck my head on a boulder by the side of the road. As I closed my eyes for the last time, I could hear my husband saying, 'No, oh no, please don't leave me.' "

Muriel looked up at Ariel.

"I didn't want to leave him but I was being pulled out of my body. The next thing I knew I was in the tunnel of light."

Ariel walked over to Muriel and gave her a hug. As she sat down, she gave the briefest of smiles.

Ariel then began to talk about the difficulty of dying a violent death.

"Most people have no understanding of what has happened to them when they die. Often times, they are thrown out of their bodies and suddenly find themselves looking down at the situation. Usually there is a great deal of blood around them, which is quite frightening. They stand around waiting for someone to come and tell them what to do. If medical help has arrived, they try to tell the doctors and nurses that they are okay. But no one seems to hear or pay any attention to them. It is as if they are in a void. Some people have even tried to get back into their bodies and are immediately assaulted with tremendous pain, which throws them out even further. No matter what idea people may have about dying, the most frightening thing is the fear of losing loved ones. Death itself is just a moment."

As I glanced at Muriel, I noticed that she was nodding her head in quiet assent. Other people seemed very somber. Ariel then continued.

"Spiritual guides are always at someone's side when their life is ended on the Earth level. Usually, if the death is a non-violent one, the person who is dying quickly sees his or her guides, sometimes even before they have left their body. Those guides then help the person to see the tunnel and go through it.

In the case of violent death, the guides are there, but because of the shock of dying so quickly, the person usually does not acknowledge the guides. Remember, the person is usually too busy trying to get the attention of the living. Sometimes, the guides have to wait until that person gets some idea of what is happening and starts to call for help. Often times the guides will gently call the person's name to try and get their attention. If they succeed, then they will immediately try to explain why no one is paying any attention to them. Sometimes, the result of that conversation is more fear because it is usually at this point that the person realizes that they have died and must now leave behind all that they have treasured and desired on Earth. A strong state of denial is the next stage that the guide has to deal with.

For the person who has just passed on, a big smack on the face comes when they see either their body being put into a body bag and placed into the coroner's wagon, or when they see their body being covered with a sheet in a hospital. If they are not watched carefully, they will immediately try to get back into their body just to try and prove to themself that they are not dead. People also have returned to their homes to talk to loved ones, who at that point in time may not even know that person has died."

Ariel smiled at this point, and continued.

"People sometimes will know that a loved one has died because they either saw or heard them bid goodbye. When that occurs, even though the news of a loved one's death is always a surprise, the shock is lessened by the advance knowledge. At this point, the most important thing is to get the person who has just died into the tunnel of light and on to the astral level so that he can sleep for whatever time is necessary. During this sleep, the person is healed of the trauma of death.

If the death has been especially violent, then that one is usually not allowed to attend their own funeral. Actually, most people are not allowed to attend their own funeral because it is too traumatic for them and their hold on the Earth level is still too strong. It would be quite difficult to bid your spouse goodbye for what may be many years. If you have children, then the goodbye would create much too much pain. Often times it is better just to let people sleep until they decide it is time to wake up, which is what happened to most of you in this room."

A gentleman stood up and asked Ariel, "What would happen if a person were better prepared for death? Would their violent death be any less traumatic?"

"If people were better educated about the death and dying process, then even in case of a violent death the person would know that the first thing they should do is call for a spiritual guide to show them the way to the tunnel of light. They would know that they should not try to get back into their body if they do not see the cord still attached between them and their physical body."

Ariel then pointed out to everyone that in most parts of the world there is great denial as to death and dying. People do not want to talk about dying. They only want to talk about living, as if they feel that they are going to live forever.

Ariel then asked, "Were any of you prepared for your death? Had any of you given any real thought as to what death might be like, and if there were a life after death?"

No one could raise their hand. They all had feared death, and had tried to avoid thinking about it at all costs, for all the good that it had done them.

I thought about my own fears and realized that until I began seeing Troy, I had no clear understanding about death. Actually, I had thought that once you turned 100 years-old you just started over again.

Troy whispered to me, "In a way, you weren't that far off."

Someone asked, "What happens when you die in your sleep?"

Ariel replied, "Most people spend time on the astral level when they are sleeping anyway. So when someone dies in their sleep, the cord is cut and they just continue sleeping on the astral level, until it is time for them to awaken."

"Are there any more questions?"

Everyone seemed lost in their own deep thoughts.

"If there are no more questions, then class is dismissed."

As people stood up to begin leaving, Ariel mentioned that the next class would deal with the beginning phases of life on this level.

Everyone smiled. A much more pleasant subject would be discussed next time.

"Troy," I asked, "where are these people going to when they leave this class?"

"Most of them will return to their homes and spend time with family and friends. In the beginning a great deal of time is spent just resting up from the labors of Earth."

"Are any of these family and friends still residing on the astral level?"

"Sometimes they are. If you want, you can wait for your loved one to arrive, especially if that arrival will be in a short time. A lot of people can and do wait. Other times family and friends will come down from whatever level they currently reside on and will stay with the new arrival until they are a bit more settled in."

"But everyone grows, right Troy?"

"Sooner or later."

As we began the return to the Earth level, I wished for a peaceful death for everyone on Earth.

"It's not possible," came Troy's reply.

He was reading my thoughts again.

"I know. But I can still wish."

"Come on, Little One. Let's get you back into your body."

As I settled back into my body I thought about what I had just learned and still wished that people could die peacefully in their own beds, even though I knew that that was an impossible wish.

"Goodnight Troy," I murmured and fell asleep before I heard his reply.

I next saw Troy about two weeks later, during the day-time. It was a bright Sunday morning and I was attending my Sunday school class. As I glanced at my teacher I noticed Troy standing directly behind him. I wondered what he was doing there. He seemed to be listening to my teacher's words very carefully. Even nodding his head in agreement at some of the words. I mentally asked him if we were going to go to the other side tonight and he said yes. I was so excited I almost forgot where I was and had to really concentrate in order to listen to the rest of the lesson.

All day after that, I felt like I was practically floating on air. When I returned home I quickly ran to my prayer corner to give thanks for all of the things in my life, both good and bad. As I gazed at the picture of Jesus on my wall, I felt such intense love from him that I forgot where I was and once again felt as if I was floating on air. Hours later, I felt a hand on my shoulder and realized that my mother was trying to awaken me from my reverie. It was time for dinner.

Later that evening as she was tucking me into bed she mentioned that when she had come up to me during my prayers she saw white light all around me. To her, the white light seemed to stream down from the religious pictures on the wall. She almost did not disturb me. As she put it, I looked so happy and at peace it almost seemed a shame to wake me. She also mentioned that when she touched me, she got a very minor electric shock.

My mother then asked me, "Are you going to see Troy tonight?"

I nodded my head yes and she again made me promise to return from my sojourn on the other side. As my mother turned to leave the room, she smiled at a spot beside my bed. My mother could see her beloved son.

"Troy," I said, "let's go."

He gathered me into his arms and off we went. I soon found myself in the tunnel of light. This time, however, we seemed to speed through it. The next thing I knew, we were standing in front of the building that housed the classrooms for this level.

As we entered the building, various people from the class said hello to me. Ariel was already in the room and as we took our seats I noticed that the room was a bit more full than last time. Some of the new people seemed very happy to be there. Ariel smiled at them and began to speak on the topic for this session.

"Most of you have been given a place to stay and have had family and friends helping you to make the adjustment.

Some of you slept for a few years, and some of you slept for only a few days. As I mentioned in an earlier class, the length of your sleep was dependent on several factors, not the least of which is, how you lived and how you died. Some of you have even been to the Hall of Records in order to review the life you just left. I hope you discovered that you yourselves are your own harshest critics.

Now, in order to help you understand who you are and where you are going you will take a series of classes. This class is just the beginning of your new adventure. As soon as you have learned all that is required you will move on to the next class. Everyone will move on to the various other classes at there own speed. There is absolutely nothing wrong with being either a fast or slow learner. The goal here is not to be the first one out of this class, but rather to understand more about yourself before you leave this class."

Ariel paused to let the group process that information. As I glanced around the room, everyone seemed to be lost in thought. But I also noticed a very quiet peace that filled the room, bringing comfort and hope to all of us. I could not believe that I was able to there, listening to these words of wisdom. I silently thanked everyone concerned who had made it possible for me to be here. The rush of love I felt at that moment overwhelmed my very soul, and I felt tears rushing to my eyes. "I love you so much, God," I said, in my heart of hearts. Thank you, thank you, thank you! As I opened my eyes, I became aware that all eyes were on me. But instead of being embarrassed, the love I felt rushed from me and I opened my arms to share it with everyone. All around me I heard thank yous and amens.

Ariel then very quietly said, "That is why we are here."

I bowed my head once again in my own silent acknowledgment of God's love and grace. It was a powerful expression of Love.

Ariel continued on by saying, "Here, on the beginning levels, we try to keep everything as similar to Earth as possible."

He smiled as he explained, "We have discovered that it is often very hard to break people's expectations and routines. Therefore, this beginning level has both day and night. People here prepare meals, and even work jobs if they desire."

Ariel laughed and said, "Usually, that part of the routine in people's lives here is the first part to drop away. The most important thing that happens on these beginning levels is a clearer understanding about life and death and the part that all of us play in this big and wonderful adventure.

"As we continue along in this afterlife, we will meet people from all different levels of understanding. Some of them are considered masters, meaning that they have mastered most of the basic knowledge about who we are and where we come from. Eventually, all of us will be masters."

Some people shook their heads in disbelief at this statement but continued to listen in awe and wonder. Ariel then nodded his head and a beautiful presence filled the room. I could not tell if the presence was male or female. But the positive energy radiating from that one was so overwhelming that the entire class was stunned into silence. It was almost too much to bear.

As Ariel smiled his approval, the presence roamed about the room, occasionally pausing in front of certain people. Troy was silent. As I glanced at Ariel, I noticed that he was staring in my direction. His glance seemed to penetrate my very being. The presence followed his glance until it hovered directly in front of me. I was filled by the magnificence of this being, so much so that I begged for more. Suddenly I was inside the presence. It was as if I no longer existed and only this loving presence mattered in the whole wide world. Time seemed to stop and nothing held importance in this moment. I heard Ariel and Troy say, Please don't take her yet. We all have so much to learn.

Suddenly the presence spoke. Its voice was music to my ears, "So be it, Ariel. She is yours for this moment. Enjoy her and help her grow and be all that she is meant to be."

I felt the presence begin to move away from me.

"Please don't go," I cried. "All of us here need your love and wisdom."

Once again I heard the voice. But this time it was laughing ever so gently.

"None of you have seen the last of me. I will return."

So saying, it slowly departed from the classroom. A great sigh went up from the room, as if a thousand voices suddenly cried out, "don't go!" Both Ariel and Troy seemed lost in deep thoughts. Without anyone saying a word, it was understood that class was over for this day.

As Troy and I stood up to leave, the room became very quiet.

"What's going on, Troy?" I asked. "I don't understand."

Troy smiled at me and said, "Please be quiet for just a little longer, Kathie. Some day you will understand."

Ariel came over to me, and placed his hand in mine. He looked deeply into my eyes. Seeming to find whatever confirmation he had been looking for, he smiled and turned away. My mind was full of unanswered questions. But they would have to wait because I felt a strong tug on my cord. Troy then picked me up and began speeding toward the tunnel.

"What's wrong, Troy?" I asked.

"Mother is trying to wake you up, and if I don't get you back right away, she may start to panic and think that you have died."

Moments later I was back in my body, safe and sound.

I heard my mother ask me, "What's wrong? Why is it taking so long for me to wake you?"

I finally opened my eyes, and took in her worried face.

"I'm okay, Mom. I just was very deep."

She looked at me as if she wasn't sure whether to believe me or not. She stared at me for a few moments longer then wearily shook her head and motioned that it was time to get up. As I dragged myself out of bed, my body seemed so very heavy.

"Mom, you don't have to worry about me staying on the other side. As wonderful as it is, I want to live here on Earth. There is a reason for all of this happening to me. I don't know what it is yet but I intend to spend my life trying to find out."

Mom looked at me and breathed an audible sigh of relief. I hoped that I had finally convinced her that, God willing, I had no intention of leaving Earth anytime soon. What I did want to do was to try to lead a better life, and to put into practice the teachings that I was learning on the other side.

6

Thoughts are Things

A FEW DAYS PASSED BEFORE I SAW TROY AGAIN. As he led
me through the tunnel of light, I thought about my last class
and the being that had visited it. Troy was unusually quiet.
I wondered if I had done something wrong, but was afraid
to ask him. Having arrived at class, I noticed that there were
several strangers talking with Ariel. Troy and I took our seats
and waited for the class to begin. I glanced around the room
and everyone seemed very subdued.

"What is going on?" I asked Troy.

He shushed me into silence. As Ariel began to speak, the
strangers remained standing with him.

"I know most of you are wondering about what is going
on up here, and now I will tell you. The people standing here
next to me will be teaching some of you in the next phase of
your learning. As your name is called by them, please come
to the front of the room and line up next to the person who
called your name."

"Am I being moved to a new class?" I whispered to Troy.

"No," he replied.

For some reason I was content with his answer. As it turned out, only a few people were actually moved to a new class. For the rest of us, it was time for our class to begin.

Ariel began by saying, "No one, whose name was not called, should feel slighted in any way."

Everyone laughed, and somehow the atmosphere in the classroom became much lighter.

"Soon, all of you will have to go to the Hall of Records. In that building you will find the Akashic Records, which lists everything that anyone has ever done.

The building is colored green because green is a very healing color. And believe me, if you are at all honest with what you are seeing, then you will need some form of healing."

"What about God judging you?" I asked.

"In a way, that is exactly what happens. Everyone has to go to the Hall of Records before they can progress onward to the other levels. In the room you go to, you will see a comfortable sofa and a large screen. Upon this screen, you will see your entire life, from start to finish. You will not be spared any detail. You will be able to see what you learned and what you didn't learn. We have learned that you are a much harsher judge than God could ever be. When you see the good things you did, and the times you took a wrong turn in life, you will understand what your life was supposed to teach you, and what you still need to learn on this level in order to continue your growth.

You will not go through this process alone. You will have someone with you who is from one of the higher planes. That being will be totally non-judgmental regarding your life. It is up to you to see and learn from the life you have left behind. How you respond to the viewing of your life will determine what you will do next on this level."

Ariel paused for a moment, then said, "Some of you will be going to the Hall of Records very soon."

That comment made the whole room go quiet. As for myself, I resolved right then and there, to lead a much better life. I knew that in all probability, my life would not be totally squeaky clean. But in the future I would try my best to make better decisions. I felt as if I had again been forewarned. As I glanced around the room, everyone seemed to be in deep thought. I didn't notice too much fear, only genuine concern for the lives everyone had just left behind. None of us were sure of what our experiences would be like in the rooms. But, we were sure that we would come away from the experience with a much better understanding of ourselves and the lives we had lived.

At this point, Ariel decided to end the class because he felt that most people had a lot to think about. As the students began to leave, Ariel and Troy asked me if I wanted to revisit the Hall of Records. At first I didn't. But then I decided that, if they were going to offer me another sneak preview, why not? Ariel waited until everyone had left. Then he and Troy walked me over to the green building known as the Hall of Records.

As I entered the building, I became aware of a mixture of energy. Some people were smiling as they left their individual rooms. Others were crying out loud about missed opportunities and challenges left unmet.

"What will happen to people whose lives were not all that they should have been?" I asked Ariel.

"They will be allowed to attend special classes, to help them learn whatever they need to learn."

Ariel then led me into one of the many rooms in the building. As I entered, I felt as if I were once again a baby being held in my mother's arms. As I made my way to the sofa, I noticed that Ariel and Troy were leaving.

"Where are you going?" I cried.

"This experience is for you, and you alone," replied Troy. "You will not see all of your short life, just a few minutes, here and there."

Both he and Ariel did not feel that I would be traumatized by anything I would see. After they left, I suddenly felt a rush of the deepest love I had ever felt, and knew that someone had entered the room to help me. As I sat down, the show appeared on the screen. I was watching a scene from one of my Sunday school classes, in which I was once again asking a lot of unanswerable questions. I noticed that my approach was not one of anger but that of an inquisitive child.

The scene then switched to a confrontation with my mother. I wanted to read my book and she wanted me to help her in the kitchen. I saw that my response was not always respectful toward the woman who had given me life. I began to thank God for this opportunity and resolved that I would give both my mother and father a great deal more respect.

I then heard a very mellow and soft voice say, "All of life teaches us things about ourselves, if we would only stop and listen."

I smiled and said, "I will try to listen to whatever life is trying to show me, in any given moment."

"That is all we ask," was the sweet response.

As I opened the door to the room, Ariel and Troy were waiting outside. They didn't ask me about what I had seen of my life. They wanted to know if I was satisfied with their technique of allowing people to view their life.

"I don't know how other people feel, but I can tell you that based upon what I have just seen, I will definitely make a change in my life. That way I can hopefully learn the lessons that my life is trying to teach me."

Both Troy and Ariel smiled, and Ariel said to Troy, "It is time to return Kathie to her body."

The next morning I told my mother about what I had seen the previous night.

"Is what you are seeing in your travels at night helping you in your life?" she asked me.

"I am trying to put into practice some of the things that I am learning on the other side."

"I like the changes I am seeing in you, and I feel comfortable with what you are doing with Troy at night."

I smiled and asked her, "Is there anything I can do to help you?"

She nodded her head yes, and we began our day together.

I next saw Troy about one month later. At the time I was contemplating getting baptized at my church.

As Troy guided me through the tunnel I asked him, "Do you think I should get baptized?"

"Will this help you feel closer to God?"

I thought about that for a moment and replied, "Yes."

"Then you have answered your own question."

His answer caused me to think more deeply about this step I wanted to take.

"Well, I don't think I need to decide this tonight."

Troy laughed.

Soon we arrived at the yellow-hued building. Troy indicated that I should take my seat while he spoke briefly to Ariel. After I sat down, I noticed that Troy and Ariel were in a deep conversation and occasionally, they would both look up at me. I suddenly felt that this would be my last class with Ariel. I immediately felt a strong sense of sorrow and began to cry. Troy finally noticed that I was crying and came over to inquire as to what was the problem. I couldn't say a word.

Finally Troy said, "Don't worry, Kathie, you will see Ariel again. I promise."

It was amazing that he knew exactly what I was upset about and immediately said just what I needed to hear. I dried my tears, and waited for the other people to arrive. Ariel began speaking after the class had settled down.

"Many of you have asked me about the houses you are currently staying in. You are wondering if you can change some aspects of the house. The class today will be about changing your house, or completely reconstructing it."

Many people began wondering out loud about how to do this. Ariel waited until the room had once again settled down into relative quiet.

"The houses here are created by the citizens of this level. The houses are usually occupied until the person moves on to a higher level. Sometimes we let the house stand so that a newcomer can occupy it, until he or she learns how to make their own house. Other times the house is removed and another is created in its place."

Ariel paused and asked, "Does anyone have any questions at this point?"

We were all intrigued, but no one wanted to interrupt him. Ariel then wrote a very simple sentence on the blackboard:

Thoughts are things.

"Does anyone have any idea what this sentence means?" asked Ariel.

Everyone shook their heads no. I looked up at Troy.

He remained quiet. I knew that this was going to be a very important class and sat up straight. I didn't want to miss anything that Ariel was going to say.

"On this level, you can do many things that might seem impossible on Earth. One of the things that you can do here is to create things seemingly out of the air."

Ariel turned and there right in front of him, was a vase with one dozen roses in it. We all jumped. "How did you do that?" we all asked in unison. Ariel smiled.

"Well, it is really quite simple. I thought about the roses, then manifested them here in the room."

Well, I thought, it really doesn't seem simple to me.

"On this level and each level thereafter, you are not bothered with a cumbersome body and the feeling that you cannot do anything magical. On Earth imagination is not given much credit. In fact sometimes people are accused of having too much of an imagination. Here too much of an imagination is usually not enough. Let's begin by having you close your eyes."

I closed my eyes and waited for more instructions.

"Try to imagine white light while keeping your eyes closed. If you can't see the white light, relax for a moment, then concentrate a little harder."

Ariel then asked us to nod our heads if we saw the white light. I nodded my head and waited for Ariel to speak again.

"Now, imagine the white light mixed with pink light."

This is fun, I thought. In fact, everyone seemed to be having a good time.

"Imagine the pink and white light merging into a beautiful rose. See the rose very clearly. Is anyone having any trouble seeing the rose?"

Since I had my eyes closed, I couldn't see if anyone was having trouble doing this little exercise. In the meantime my rose was growing a stem, complete with thorns.

"Some of you are having a little problem with this exercise and are going to be taken into another classroom for some basic training in visualization. Open your eyes and rest for a moment."

Those who could not do the exercise left the room. Ariel assured the rest of us that they would return in a few days following some very basic instruction and a little encouragement.

"Don't worry about the people who had to leave. Removing them was no slight. They just need more time in which to do the exercise and Ariel did not want them to become frustrated," whispered Troy.

Ariel then turned his attention back to all of us.

"Okay, let's try it again. Please try to resume exactly where you left off."

I closed my eyes and once again could see the light pink rose with a long stem.

"Now, whatever image you are seeing, try to change it into an orange."

My rose began to form into an orange.

"If you can now see the orange, raise your hands."

I raised my hand.

"Now, try to take the next step. Hold your hands out in front of you and feel the orange in your hands."

I took a deep breath and held out my hands. Instantly, the orange was gone from my gaze, and I could feel it in my hands. I opened my eyes and, sure enough, there was an orange sitting in my hands. I looked around the room and saw other people with oranges in their hands also. Someone laughed, and suddenly the whole room exploded into laughter. We had been able to do this on our first try.

"Congratulations! Now, you know how to build your house on this level."

"Wait a minute," someone said. "An orange is a small thing. How do you expect us to be able to build something as large as a house?"

Ariel smiled and replied, "I expect you to build it the same way you created the orange. Start with any color of light and try creating little things until you feel comfortable enough to start manifesting larger items. Remember what I wrote on the blackboard at the beginning of this class. Thoughts are things. On this level, whatever you think about can come true. Therefore if you want to build a house then just pick out the area and imagine your house sitting there. If you have faith in yourself, then your house will magically appear. If you can't do it on your first, second, or third try, just keep trying. Don't give up!"

I glanced around the room and could feel the excitement. Everyone seemed as if they wanted to leave the room immediately and create their very own house. As I sat thinking about the class, I wondered if I could do this on the earthly plane.

"Ariel," I asked, "can people on Earth do this?"

"Yes. But it is more difficult there because most people believe that the Earth level is the only reality and just cannot seem to let go of their earthly beliefs. Also, things tend to go much more slowly there. In order to have your thoughts produce these wonders you must be really, really patient. But don't worry, Kathie, there will be other classes for you so that you can learn more about this topic."

With those words said, I knew this class was over. After everyone in the classroom left, Ariel approached me.

"Well, Little One, this is the last class you will have with me for a little bit. It is now time for you to move on to other classes where you will learn more about earthly and afterlife living."

"Ariel," I cried, "I don't want to go to another class. I want you to be my teacher."

He gave me a hug and whispered into my ear that he would see me again. He would sit-in on some of my upcoming classes so that I would not lose touch with him.

I then smiled and said, "Thank you, Ariel, for all that you have shown me. I look forward to seeing you again in the very near future."

Troy then thanked Ariel for his time and promised him that he would take good care of me.

"I'll bring her back from time to time," said Troy.

"No, Troy," said Ariel. "In the future, I must go to her."

"Then, so be it," said Troy.

I could not make heads or tails of this conversation, but felt that all of this was happening for my highest good.

"Okay," said Troy, "I must get her back."

As I left the classroom I gave a backward glance to Ariel, who seemed to be crying.

"Troy," I said, "I don't understand. Why is Ariel crying?"

"Parting is such sweet sorrow," replied Troy. "Ariel will miss you."

"I'll miss him," I replied. "But I will see him again, right Troy?"

Troy laughed and nodded his head yes.

I ran back and gave Ariel a big hug.

Ariel then said, "Just think of me and I will be with you."

"Okay," I said.

As Troy led me back through the tunnel of light, I was both sad and happy. I was sad because a change was being made in my life and I would no longer be sitting in Ariel's classes. I was happy because the thought of what I might learn from future classes was both frightening and uplifting. Troy and I arrived back into my room. Then he assisted me in getting back into my body.

He then said, "I will be back for you in about one month," he promised.

"Okay Troy. I love you, and thank you for doing this for me."

Troy then hugged me and left. Just before I fell asleep, I mentally called for Ariel and thanked him one last time.

"You're welcome," I heard him say.

7

In My Father's House

ONE MONTH LATER, I HEARD TROY'S VOICE.

"Let's go, Little One."

"Hi Troy. Are we going back to Ariel's class?"

"No," Troy laughed, "we are going to a new class. Have you forgotten so soon, Little One?"

"No, I just want to see Ariel again."

"Someday you will. But not right now."

Nothing more was said as we began to travel through the tunnel of light. We arrived at the valley surrounded by mountains and Troy took me to his house. I was about to ask him a question when he motioned for me to be silent. I wondered why he was waiting to take me to my next class. All of a sudden a presence arrived. I remained motionless while Troy greeted his visitor and asked if I was really ready. The being nodded yes, and then spoke to me for the first time.

"Hi Kathie. My name is Aurora, and I am to be your next teacher."

"Hello Aurora. Will my next class be here in Troy's house?"

"No, I am going to take you to a higher level of this plane."

I fell silent. She gathered me up in her arms. I felt a slight movement and then I heard the most melodious sounds I had ever heard.

"Where am I?" I asked.

Aurora told me that I was on the highest level of the astral plane, where her classes were conducted. I looked around for Troy and was comforted to see him standing near me. Aurora motioned for me to follow her. She seemed to glide above the ground. I wondered why she was not walking, but kept my question to myself. We soon arrived at a rather small building. Aurora went into this building and as I followed her, I noticed for the first time that the building was glowing golden-yellow. I could not believe my eyes. As I went in I noticed that the classrooms were all quiet. I could tell that there were people inside each room. But, there was not any noise coming from any of them.

We then entered one of the rooms with nine other students all waiting patiently for Aurora to arrive. They nodded their heads respectfully as she entered the room. I took a seat toward the back of the room and Troy sat down beside me.

Aurora began by saying, "This will be the last class you will take before moving on to the next level."

I glanced at Troy and was puzzled because I did not feel that I was ready for this.

He looked at me and whispered, "You should not feel afraid. This class is where you need to be at this moment."

I returned my attention to Aurora.

A student asked her, "How many levels are there?"

"There are many levels, and each level is a plane unto itself."

Aurora then began to name some of the various levels:
1. Physical or Earth plane
2. Astral plane
3. Mental plane
4. Buddhic-Intuitional plane
5. Spiritual-Nirvanic plane
6. Monadic plane
7. Divine plane
8. Unmentionable No-Name planes

"Each of these planes will be discussed in future classes. But right now, I need to remind you about the colors around your bodies called the aura. Each of you has your own individual colors, which reflect your spiritual growth and what you are feeling in each moment. Your aura indicates which plane you belong on."

I sat up startled. So that was what I had been seeing around people—auras. It was nice to finally have a name for what I had seen all my life. I had always inwardly known when people were happy or sad because of the colors. I wasn't sure what each color meant but had a strong feeling about what I thought they meant. I believed that everyone could see these colors. Now, I knew that that was not the case.

Aurora began looking around the room. Her eyes settled on me for the briefest of moments. She smiled and then asked for another student to join her at the front of the classroom. She asked him to take a deep breath and think positive thoughts. She then asked us to look, but not look, at the student. I looked at him and noticed that the colors swirling around him were really nice pastels.

Aurora then asked, "Does anyone see the colors around him?"

No one raised their hands at first. Then one student did. She mentioned that she saw pastel colors around him. I nodded my head in agreement. Aurora then indicated that we were seeing correctly.

"For most people," said Aurora, "their aura extends about one to two feet away from their body. In someone who is leading a spiritual life, their aura can extend anywhere from one or two feet to twenty feet or more."

I wanted to ask Aurora what the purpose is of having a large aura but felt that, at this point in time, I should just listen to her.

"The colors that surround each of us are a reflection of our spiritual development and our emotional state. These colors are especially meaningful once you leave your bodies behind and come and reside on this level. As you are well aware, all of you have been attending classes that are helping you to learn about the type of lives you led while on Earth, and the type of lives you could have lived. We can tell where you are in your development by the colors that are reflected in your aura."

Aurora then asked, "Does anyone have any questions at this time?"

No one raised their hand, so I did.

"Aurora," I asked, "I have always seen colors around people, and I have always wondered what the various colors meant?"

"I will not be giving you a description of what the colors mean because that has been taught to everyone else in earlier classes. Kathie, you will get that exact information at a later time. Instead, I will describe how we can use our auras to travel on to the next levels."

Just before she began, Troy said, "You will learn all about the aura in future classes. Since you can see them with complete clarity, there is no need for you to take any of the basic aura classes right now."

I listened in amazement as Aurora described what we would need to do to travel to the next level of existence.

"By now, all of you have had classes where you learned how to use your will to create and uncreate whatever you needed on this level. Now, I want you to take those lessons one step further."

"Each of you arrived here through the death of your physical body. Now, in order to continue on your path of growth, you will have to leave your astral bodies on this level and ascend into your mental bodies."

Many of us turned and looked at each other. Fear was evident on most faces.

Aurora laughed and said, "I see you have become too comfortable in your astral bodies and are reluctant to move on."

One gentleman raised his hand. He was concerned about leaving his wife behind on the astral level, as she had recently arrived on this level and he had stayed behind to be with her. Aurora assured him that, as soon as his wife had learned the lessons that she needed to learn, he would be allowed to rejoin her on this level, and could help her to make the next transition.

I, on the other hand, was brimming with questions. I raised my hand and inquired if I could ask Aurora a question. She replied yes.

"Aurora, I am confused. If we have to 'die' to this level to move on to the next plane, then how are we able to return to our 'dead' astral bodies? I mean, no one can return to their physical body after death. So how is it that we can return to our astral bodies?"

All of the students nodded their heads. Apparently they were wondering the same thing.

"All of your bodies are within you. Each time you need one you put it on, as if you were putting on a new dress or a new pair of pants."

"Where do you put this body on?" I asked.

"Well, when did you put on your astral body when you traveled here?"

I thought long and hard about this question. I did not recall putting on an astral body, per se. It was as if everything I needed was provided for automatically.

Aurora laughed and said, "That is the key, Little One. While one is being folded and put away, the other one is being slipped into place. It is as easy as thinking about it."

I then remembered the class in which Ariel had taught us how to visualize a rose and thereby create it at the same time. No sooner had Ariel thought about the rose than it had appeared. We all had tried to manifest various items. Sometimes successfully, sometimes not so successfully.

Troy then asked me, "Do you recall seeing anyone looking either younger or older than when you saw them last?"

"Why, yes. But I was so busy trying to absorb and learn all that I could, I never paid much attention to how people looked on any given day. However, from time to time, I did notice that certain people seemed to be aging or getting younger at the various times that I saw them."

Troy then said, "You can appear as any age you wish to be."

Before I could completely absorb that notion, Aurora

then went on to say, "As a matter of fact, you can appear as anything you wish to be."

Whereupon she disappeared from sight briefly, then reappeared as a young man. She startled all of us by how quickly she was able to do this.

"All of you must be able to do this before you can journey on," said Aurora.

We sat in silence and I thought back to the beginning of this class. The beings here could tell if we were ready to go on by what they saw in our auras. But somehow or other, we had to be able to release ourselves from our astral bodies, manifest our mental bodies or whatever plane is next, and then cross some invisible barrier in order to move on. It was all too much for me to take in at that moment. Yet I felt as if I already knew how to do these things, and with some practice, I would be able to take this next step. Others in the class were looking very doubtful.

Aurora then shouted, "It will be your doubts, and only your doubts, that will keep you from moving on. At our next session, we will practice your visualization skills and see if anyone can indeed move out of their astral bodies."

As Troy and I walked away, I thought about all that I had just learned. It was hard to think about dying to this level.

"Troy," I said, "I thought that once you had suffered your physical death there would be no more dying."

Troy picked me up, and looked me square in the face.

"It is not about dying, Little One. It is about growing and releasing all of the things you do not need."

Suddenly, a thought dawned in my mind.

"Troy, you do not normally live on this plane, right?"

"Right."

THE BIRTH CALLED DEATH

"Then you had to 'come down' from another level in order to be here with me."

"That is correct, Kathie."

"Then, did you have to die to all of the other levels that you had to travel through?"

"Actually, Kathie, it doesn't quite work that way, and there are no words to actually describe the experience. Suffice it to say, that you will know exactly what we mean when we use the term 'die' in relationship to traveling between the various levels here. But now, it is time to get you back. I'll return for you at the end of your next day."

What a strange way to put that, I thought, as we once again rushed through the tunnel of light. Troy settled me into my body and bade me goodnight. I was asleep before I could even say goodnight in return.

The next day I reflected on all that I had learned on the previous night. I couldn't wait to return to Aurora's class. The day seemed to pass by so slowly. Eventually, mom was tucking me into bed after I had said my nightly prayers.

A little bit later, I was again sitting in the classroom with Troy. Aurora came in and began by asking all of us to stand up. She walked around the classroom, glancing at all of us. As she called out various names, additional people came into the room and stood alongside those whose names had been called. Imagine my surprise when Ariel came and stood alongside of me, after my name had been called. Soon, each person in the room had been joined by another being. As I glanced at Ariel, Troy was nowhere to be found.

Before I could begin to get upset, I heard Ariel's soothing words, "Please don't worry, Kathie, Troy will be right back. He had to go back to Earth, to attend to another one of your mother's relatives."

"Who?"

"Your Uncle Henry."

Uncle Henry, I thought. I had just seen him three days ago when he showed up suddenly at our doorstep for a short visit. He had told my mom that he had just felt a strong urge to see us again. His was a wonderful visit, full of stories about their childhood and their good and sad times together. Now, he too was gone from the earth level. Even though, I felt that I should be sad, somehow I just couldn't feel bad for him. His wonderful adventure was just beginning for real.

Ariel brought me back to reality with a gentle tap on my arm.

"Pay attention, Kathie. This will be very important."

As I turned my attention back to Aurora, I heard her asking if anyone could imagine a rose. All of us raised our hands.

"Good! Now, can you smell the rose?"

That was a little bit tougher, but most of us raised our hands. Aurora was silent for a moment. She seemed to be concentrating so we went silent as well. Suddenly, I felt myself surrounded by the smell of a beautifully scented rose. It was so pure that I was totally awed by it. As I began to focus on the rose's scent, I seemed to become more and more surrounded by the rose. It was as if nothing in the world existed but the rose. As I felt myself become drawn into the rose, it seemed as if there was no difference between myself and the rose. I could not tell where the rose ended and I began. As I gave myself up to this process, I began to spread my petals, extending myself outward. I was blooming and all of the glory and beauty of this rose was a great sight to behold. I felt a tugging at my base. Someone, or something, was trying to stop this process from completing itself. A voice was whispering a name that no longer had any meaning to this little one. I could hear the coursing of a mighty river, its golden water beckoning me to become one with it. Its pounding surge of water filling my entire being with its radiant golden light. Other voices became more insistent, one in particular, which I barely recognized. The rose began to fade into my very being. In its place was a beautiful ball of the purest light, which had flowed out of me. In it was the very essence of joy, peace, and love.

"Little One, Little One, Little One."

These two words, were repeated over and over until I was able to totally focus on them. I called out to Troy, his voice becoming my anchor. As I gradually re-oriented myself to a position nearer to Troy, I felt an incredible sense of peace.

Many eyes were on me. Aurora stood next to me.

She asked me, "Do you remember any of what just happened to you?"

"Yes."

As I turned to glance around the room, other students were in various stages of being both in and out of their astral bodies. Good, I thought, I am not the only one. As the rest of the class began to settle down, there were excited murmurs all over the room. I was stunned. The room had a whole different level of energy in it.

Aurora commended everyone on how well they had done. She then divided up the class into blocks of fours and eights. Aurora stated that some of the people were ready to depart their astral bodies right now and would be sent back to their astral homes to do whatever they needed to do before their upcoming departure. Others, needed more practice and would be sent to a different room in the school building to help them grow more slowly.

Everyone was sent away at the same time, except for Troy, Ariel, and myself. No one wanted to speak at first, and then suddenly everyone began talking at once. Ariel and Aurora began by saying that they both wanted to journey with me to the next level. Troy nodded his head in agreement. All three seemed very concerned about something that I was not understanding.

Aurora then asked me, "At any time did you sense that the rose was not a part of you?"

"No. I was the rose, and the rose was me."

Ariel then asked me to once again visualize a rose.

"Why? Am I doing something wrong?"

No, all three replied.

"We just need to see if what you experienced was because of you or because of the class," replied Ariel.

"Please, Kathie," Troy said, "try to imagine the rose again."

I didn't understand why they were so concerned, but, since I was their guest, I did as they asked. I closed my eyes and imagined myself holding a rose. I could see all of the petals forming into a complete flower. I opened my eyes to see if the rose was inside or outside of myself. It was in front of me. I glanced around to see if Troy, Ariel, or Aurora was watching me and discovered that I was alone. I didn't know if I should try to continue, but thought, "What the heck." The rose shimmered in front of me, its beautiful petals gleaming with color and light. As I walked around it, I could see that it was perfectly formed. I noticed that a wonderful scent was coming from the rose. I was almost afraid to go near it, and could not believe that such a beautiful flower could have come from my own thoughts. The scent of the rose began to carry me away. I decided to see if the rose was solid so I walked into it. It surrounded me in much the same way as the earlier rose had. I was the rose. Growing tall, strong, and pure. As I thought about this wonderful transformation, I wondered what my other bodies looked like. Then I remembered the ball of light that I had experienced earlier. "Was that it?" I thought, "Why not?" I began to visualize the rose as being a small ball of light and I watched as the rose began to pull itself inward and, at the same time, spread itself outward, as a beautiful pulsating pink ball of light. I felt like laughing as I directed the ball of light to move about the room. I danced as I had never danced before moving around the room with such grace and freedom of movement that I immediately understood how to move around on the higher levels. I felt myself drawn upward and inward toward something or someone that I could not begin to understand. Even while I was thinking these thoughts, I, as the ball of light, was continuing my dance around the room, which I suddenly realized was no longer there. It seemed as if I had entered a void.

"Troy," I cried.

"I'm right here beside you, Little One."

"Where am I?"

Troy laughed.

"You are here."

"Where is here, Troy?"

Again I heard Troy laugh as he exclaimed, "Now, that is a good question!"

"Are Ariel and Aurora still here, wherever here is?"

I heard both of them laugh and say, "Yes, we are still all together."

"Kathie," Troy asked, "do you think that you can form your eyes to help you adjust to this level?"

"Of course I can," I said, rather indignantly.

I opened my eyes and immediately closed them again. What I saw was absolutely unbelievable to me. Colors unlike any I had ever seen anywhere, on any level, were present everywhere. I tried to see if I could see what this new body looked like and soon realized that I had become a ball of light. Almost at once, the first thing I wanted to do was to dance around the universe.

I felt, what could only be called, a restraining hand somewhere upon me. Then I heard Ariel say, "Perhaps you should be returned to Earth now. You need to absorb this new body and this new world into your being."

Troy helped me to re-assume my astral body and begin my journey back to Earth.

As I began to enter my body, Troy said, "It will be about a month before I will be able to come and get you again."

"Why?"

"I need to check something in the Akashic Records. Then, a decision needs to be made as to whether or not you will be allowed to continue your visits."

I began to cry and Troy said to me, "I assure you that all will be well, and just remember that, it will be God's will, not yours, that will be done."

I thanked him for his timely reminder and told him that I would wait for his return.

During the month that I didn't see Troy, I tried to understand all that I had experienced on the other side of life, as I now called it. It seemed to me that each moment of our lives teaches us something about ourselves, if we would only just listen. But there is the rub: how to listen to what life is trying to show us.

I hoped that, if I were allowed to continue my visits, I would learn how to listen. I tried to be patient, and spent a lot of time in my prayer corner praying that, whatever happened it would be God's will. To my mom I seemed to be very inward and withdrawn during that time period. She was very concerned for my well being, but for the wrong reasons. She was afraid that I was preparing to die. Little did she know that I was preparing to live.

"Hello Troy," I said, exactly one month later.

Troy's greeting to me was one of sheer joy.

"Hello Little One."

"I see that you have come back. Is it time to continue my classes?"

"Oh, yes. But not in the way that you are anticipating."

"What do you mean, Troy?"

He stared at me for a moment. Then just said, "Let's go."

Without any further questions, I leapt out of my body and found myself on the mental level.

"Troy, where are you?" I asked.

No answer came as I stood in a scene so beautiful it brought tears to my eyes. I tried to make sense of what I was seeing. Light within form and form within light. Then I felt a pulsating vibration and instantly felt the need to become light. As I became this light, I once again felt myself expanding. The need to grow was so overwhelming that I just had to allow it to happen. The light form, which I had become, began to increase at a faster and faster pace. Where would this end, I wondered? Then, I felt another presence, one that I had not felt since that day in Ariel's class. This time I knew that I would now be allowed to go with this presence.

I both felt and heard its thoughts, as it said, "Come with me, Little One."

"Yes." I replied, even as I felt myself moving faster and faster.

The next moment I was in front of a building unlike any I had seen previously in all of these journeys. As I glanced around, I noticed that the vibrational sounds I was hearing were different than all the sounds I had heard previously. Someone called my name, so I turned to see a beautiful angelic being standing in front of me. I could not believe what I was seeing.

"Where am I?" I asked.

The being said nothing, though she motioned for me to enter the building. Just like before, I saw many doors once I stepped inside the building. All around I could hear what sounded to me like angel choruses. The angel I was following pointed to a door which swung open. I stepped inside to a very small room. Several people were already inside and greeted me warmly. I sat down next to one of the people and just waited for whatever was to happen next.

Suddenly I heard a female voice say, "In my Father's house there are many mansions."

I turned to look in the direction that the voice was coming from, and there stood the most radiant light form I could ever possibly hope to see. I was awestruck. My next thought was, I must have made a wrong turn somewhere because I was obviously in the wrong place. I heard the sound of tinkling bells. She was laughing.

"Since some of you are very new here I am going to use my voice to communicate with you. All of you are here because this is where you need to be for your next level of development," said the angel.

"Where is here?," I thought.

I then heard her say, "Does it matter where 'you' are localized, Little One?"

I thought about that for a moment.

"No, not really, I suppose. I just would like to know."

"Why is it so important?"

"It's not. But, could you please explain to me how I ended up on the Buddhic level?"

She smiled like a thousand sunbeams.

"Good. You should be able to detect wherever you are just based on your intuition."

"My intuition?"

Oh, I realized, this level is the level of intuition. The direct knowing of whatever knowledge you may need or require.

How, I wondered, did I get to this level? It did not seem as if I had taken enough classes to be here. I glanced around the room and noticed that the other people in the room seemed very content.

My new teacher then said to me, "You do indeed belong in my class."

Any protests I may have had died with the sweet sound of her voice.

I once again heard her say, "'In my Father's house, there are many mansions.' This level is just one of many."

I thought about what she was saying. The words were from the New Testament of the Bible, as spoken by Jesus. It was interesting to me how Jesus declared that God's house consisted of mansions. I had always thought of mansions as being very large houses, filled with all kinds of beautiful things and plenty of space to put those things. All of the levels I had seen were by far more beautiful than anything I had seen on Earth. Yet, each of these levels were mansions in the House of God. As I had these thoughts, the voice of my new teacher broke through. Her name was Alexandra.

"On this level, knowledge is power. Intuition is the

awareness of knowledge directly from the source of all knowledge. To be in touch with your intuition is to be in touch with power. There are many levels within this level and each one gained gives you greater and greater contact with your intuition."

Some of this was a little over my head, or so I thought, since I certainly did not feel that I was in touch with my intuition.

"Of course," continued Alexandra, "this level is called the Buddhic or intuitional level, but it is not just about intuition. This is the level where you start to become much more than you thought you could be. This is the level where all of your previous classes come together and you shed all thoughts of just being human. You are so much more than that."

I wanted to ask Alexandra so many questions. But, just as I was about to open my mouth, she dismissed the class and asked that everyone go within themselves to think about what she had said.

Troy asked me, "Do you want to meet Alexandra?"

"Yes."

Troy introduced me to Alexandra and she commented that no introduction was necessary. I wanted to ask her so many questions, but could not form the words. Instead, I closed my eyes and literally drank in her presence. As I stood in front of her, I could see how truly beautiful she really was, inside and out. Suddenly, I had a glimpse of her true form; the one she uses when she dwells on some of the higher levels, above the one where we were currently standing. This was true intuition. In that instant, I knew more about Alexandra than she could have possibly told me. Troy somehow sensed that I was in danger of becoming more than I should be at that moment, because he immediately swept me into his arms.

The next thing I knew I was being deposited into my body.

"Troy, will I see Alexandra again?"

"Of course you will."

But, somehow I sensed that my time with Alexandra was short, and I had just about used-up all of that time.

"No you haven't," Troy laughed and said. "Believe me, Alexandra would like to spend more time with you. But that is not possible at this time."

I figured I was about to get a new teacher. It seemed to me that my time spent in each of these classes was getting shorter and shorter.

Troy laughed again.

"Actually, your next class on the Buddhic level will be much longer and I am sure that you will enjoy all of those upcoming classes."

I glanced at Troy's face. He seemed so serious.

"Kathie, all of this is serious business. There are many things that you need to learn, that will help you in your adult life."

"Troy, I am ready and willing to learn all that I need to learn."

"Good."

I smiled and he smiled back at me.

As he turned to leave he said to me, "Remember all that you have learned so far and try to make it a part of your life."

"Okay."

Troy said, adding "I'll be back to get you again soon."

8

At His Feet

IT HAD BEEN SEVERAL MONTHS since I last saw Troy. Although I was eager to continue my after-death adventures, I had learned that these things moved at their own speed. Whatever was next would happen in its own good time.

Meanwhile, I went about my life trying to live out what I had learned on the other side. I became baptized in my church and was trying to immerse myself into a more devotional way of living. I spent much more time in the prayer corner in my room. My mom began to notice my intense devotion to God, but did not try to interfere. She knew that she had nothing to fear in the way of my leaving the Earth plane for good. At my young age, I was content and happy here on this level.

"Little One, Little One," said Troy.

I blinked my eyes and saw Troy standing at the end of my bed.

"Hello Troy," I said.

He smiled at me and held out his hand. I placed my hand in his and leapt out of my body.

"Are you ready for the greatest adventure of all?" asked Troy.

I smiled my reply and off we went. Again we went through the tunnel to the beautiful valley that was surrounded by mountains.

"Troy, are we starting all over again?"

"No, we are just going to pick-up an old friend, who will journey with us to the higher levels."

"Is it Ariel?"

"Of course it is!"

My heart was overjoyed at the thought of seeing Ariel again. Soon we were once again in his classroom. But this time it was empty. There seemed to be an air of expectancy. Ariel appeared and greeted me with a great big bear-hug.

"Little One," said Ariel, "oh, how I have missed you!"

"How can that be, Ariel?" I asked. "You can see me at any time. You can even come to Earth and be around me any time you like."

Ariel and Troy gave each other a look.

"Little One, yes, that is true. But sometimes we are not allowed to go to the Earth level just to check on old friends. I have my duties here, and you have your life there," replied Ariel.

"Well," I said, "I guess I'll just have to visit you here more often."

Both Ariel and Troy laughed and said, "Yes, you can do that, Kathie."

"Where are we going today, Troy?" I asked.

"Someplace very special, where you will learn a great many lessons."

"Will I attend many classes at this special place?"

"You will attend as many as you need to at this time."

"Okay, let's go!" I said.

This time Ariel picked me up and off we went. Through the various levels, I could see and feel myself discarding the bodies I did not need. It was such a strange sensation; almost like taking off a heavy layer of winter clothing. Each time a body was discarded I felt lighter and lighter, and experienced an incredible feeling of freedom. I thought about the rose that was lying deep within me, just waiting to blossom and become a ball of light.

"Oh no you don't!" said Troy. "This is not the time or the place to bring out the rose. I will let you know when you can do that."

"Troy, it is not nice to peek into private thoughts."

I heard his laughter, and he replied, "There is no privacy here."

I was scandalized. "What do you mean there is no privacy here?"

"Here there is no need for privacy because there is nothing to hide."

I thought about that for a moment. I could see and understand what he was talking about. But still, it made me very uncomfortable.

"Nevertheless, Troy, please keep out of my thoughts."

He had read my thoughts one time too many.

"I'll try to respect your 'privacy.' But that will be hard since I can see everything about you in your aura."

"You can't see everything about her, Troy. For if you could, you would be responding to her very differently," I heard Ariel say.

"Yeah!" I said.

Ariel gave me a stern look, and Troy looked confused.

"Is there something I don't know about, Ariel?" asked Troy.

"Yes, there is. But all will be revealed in good time, and you will be very pleased."

I knew better than to ask Ariel what all of that meant. I just wanted to get to my next class.

"Can we continue our journey now?" I asked both of them.

Of course, they replied in unison.

Soon we arrived at our destination. I knew immediately that we were once again on the Buddhic level. The building we now stood in front of was bathed in the most glorious shade of pink I had ever seen. It was as if the very building itself was an emanation of love, the very foundation of all that could be considered pure love. I could not believe that I was actually going to be allowed to enter this building. I was totally awestruck.

Quickly, I was guided into the building. I floated along until I reached the designated area. Soon I was standing in front of a door, which gradually swung open. The room inside was small and had several chairs grouped around a center chair. No one was inside when I stepped in but I wasn't alone for very long. Others began to arrive. There was an air of expectancy and I waited quietly with Troy and Ariel, to see what would happen next. I did not have to wait long.

The teacher appeared out of nowhere. He motioned for all of us to sit down. Then He Himself sat down very quietly and was silent for a few moments. When I got a closer look at Him, I could not believe my eyes. I immediately stood up and tried to leave the room. There was absolutely no way I belonged in this room with this teacher. I actually made it as far as the door before I felt a gentle tap on my shoulder and turned around to actually stare into the face of Jesus, for indeed it was Him.

"Where are you going, Little One?" He asked.

I stammered out my reply, "I don't belong here with you. There must be some great big mistake."

"There is no mistake. You are right where you are supposed to be."

"But I am not worthy enough to be here with you."

His laugh was like the simultaneous ringing of every church bell in the world.

"If you do not belong here with me, Little One, then where do you belong? Down below, perhaps?"

I shook my head no. I really did not think that I belonged down below.

"Little One, come and sit down with the rest of us. Surely you can do that for me."

"Of course I can," I replied, and sat down with the others.

He also sat down and was silent. I closed my eyes tightly and wondered what I would see when I opened them again. I just could not believe that I had done anything to deserve the honor that was being bestowed upon me.

"Suffer little children, and forbid them not to come unto me: for of such is the Kingdom of Heaven," said Jesus.

I raised my head and looked into his eyes. He was telling me that I did indeed belong here with Him in this class. His face was the very embodiment of love. His voice, the embodiment of truth. Ariel and Troy both glanced at me, indicating that I was where I needed to be. I settled down and listened to the words of the Master.

"What is the truth about little children?" asked Jesus.

"Why is it easier for them to come unto me in Heaven?"

His glance around the room showed me that He expected someone to answer his question. I kept my head down, as I did not dare to look into his eyes. I did not belong here, as far as I was concerned, and felt that the less noticed I was the better. When I thought that his glance had traveled on past me, I glanced up, only to find Him staring straight into my eyes. His eyes were full of love and understanding.

"Little One," asked Jesus, "why do you think Heaven is full of children?"

The thoughts in my mind were whirling at a thousand words a minute. Did I dare answer?

"Jesus, my Master, children have about them the qualities of innocence, expectation, and a genuine desire to know and be. They are full of wonder and joy, and they are uncomplicated. They ask questions and seek answers out of a sincere desire to know, without any of the guile normally associated with adults."

After I finished my answer, I wondered where all of that had come from.

"Little One, your answer is a good one."

I thought about what He had just said and more of what was happening to me began to make sense. So did his calling me Little One. In all of this, I was a child; a child who desired answers to many of the basic questions of life. A child who had gained a little understanding about life because of her adventures on the other side of death.

Jesus nodded his head in agreement and said, "Verily I say unto you, whosoever shall not receive the Kingdom of God as a little child, he shall not enter herein. The attitude of a child is the purest expression of love. It is full and complete surrender to each moment. That attitude prevails here in Heaven because surrender to the will of my Father is the highest expression of love. Any adult who cannot love or surrender, will not be able to attain the very heights of Heaven."

Jesus became silent again. Each of us in the room began to concentrate on his words, allowing them to sink in and become our very being.

To enter Heaven, we must all be as little children—full of love and life — no deceit, no untruths, just full and complete surrender to God, the Father. At that moment, my understanding and devotion grew by leaps and bounds.

Jesus began speaking again, using familiar words from the Bible. My mind was smashed to pieces, as my heart listened to his words. I still could not believe that I was sitting near the Son of God. My eyes were beholding his divine presence. What does this all mean, I wondered? How could I, a sinner, be sitting at the feet of the most holiest of masters? My heart felt dark and heavy, even though I was sitting with the Master. Then I heard his sweet voice say to me my favorite passage in the Bible.

"Let not your heart be troubled: ye believe in God, believe also in me. In my Father's house are many mansions: if it were not so, I would have told you. I go to prepare a place for you. And if I go and prepare a place for you, I will come again, and receive you unto myself; that where I am there may ye be also."

I glanced into his eyes. Their message of love and healing cleansed and purified my soul. He stood up, and all of us in the room stood up also. As we faced Him, He began to rise from the floor of the room. Everyone backed up and began to leave the room. I too turned to go, and was stopped by his voice.

"Kathie, do not go yet."

I turned to face Him again. He was now about a foot off the floor. His body was wrapped in white light, and shone with a brilliance that was almost unbearable to look at.

He held his arms open and said, "Come to me."

My mind screamed no, that I was not worthy at all. But my heart knew better. I took three steps toward Him, and felt myself embraced by his light and his love. In that embrace was the most peace and love I had ever felt. I fell to his feet, crying out my joy. My arms encircled his legs as I held onto Him; and in my heart swore that I would never let go of Him.

"Do not cry, Little One. Thou art in my protection. No harm shall come to thee. Thou art a child of my Father, in whose Love you will always dwell."

My soul felt pure. As I bent my head down to kiss the Master's feet, I knew that my journey through life, no matter how long or how difficult, would be better because of this moment. My surrender to Jesus was complete. His voice so sweet in my ear, His love so pure in my heart, made me want to do only His works. I melted into His heart and knew no more.

Two months passed before I saw Troy again. During that time I spent most of my free waking moments in the prayer corner in my room. I did not understand why or how I was being gifted with these experiences. But I did know that I wanted to surround myself in prayer with the love of Jesus. Many times, while gazing at his picture, I would see pink and white light streaming out of the picture. Then I would enter a place of stillness, and in that stillness would be the love of Jesus. It was during one of these times that I once again felt Troy's presence.

"Hello," said Troy.

"Troy," I cried, "if you are here to take me back to the other side, I do not feel that I am ready to go."

"Kathie, why do you feel that you are so unworthy of these experiences?"

I thought about his question, and was about to come up with my usual response about being a sinner, when he cut through my thoughts and said, "You are a child, and as such, are always welcomed."

"Troy, does this mean that when I become an adult I will no longer be able to have these experiences?"

"No, Little One, you will always be a child."

"What does that mean, Troy?"

"It means that one day you will totally understand this conversation and agree with me."

I let it drop, knowing that he was probably right. Now I do understand just what he was talking about.

"Are you ready to go with me now?" asked Troy.

"Yes, Troy," I answered, as I felt myself begin to rise above my body.

As I held on to Troy's hand, I instantly noticed that we were standing in front of the building that I had last seen Jesus in. Troy glanced at me, as if to calm my fears. Feeling nothing but love, I entered the building and re-entered the classroom that I had been in before. Ariel was already there and smiled at me as I took a seat next to him. Soon, other students began to arrive and we all sat in prayerful silence, until the Master appeared.

He did not speak to us at first, as He too sat down. In the silence that followed, I felt overwhelmed with the pureness of the love that was emanating from Jesus; so much so that I began to cry. Silently at first, until I felt a hand upon my head.

Then loudly, as I could not contain my joy. No words were spoken but I heard Jesus, in my heart and mind, telling me that all was well. When I could open my eyes, I discovered that I was all alone in the room. Everyone had left, even the Master. I did not understand why and was at first concerned that my crying had driven everyone away.

Then I decided that this was an opportunity for me to grow, so I stayed calm, and waited for what came next. Thus, I began to retreat into the silence. I closed my eyes and began to see white light all around me, followed by pink light, which began to surround me. I felt myself grow lighter and lighter until it seemed as if I did not exist anymore. I had become a point of light. In that point, I could sense all of mankind; their woes and worries began to pull at me, until I felt myself start to grow larger.

I asked Jesus to send his love to all of mankind, to ease their burden of suffering and pain. Suddenly, I felt his response. His Love was like a bolt of lightening sent directly to all who were in need, giving each person exactly what they needed. For myself, I asked nothing. I was content.

As I opened my eyes, I noticed that everyone had returned. We sat in the silence for a little while, until once again I heard the Master's voice.

"I am the way, the truth and the life: no man cometh unto the Father but by me."

Once again, we sat in silence. What does all of this mean, I wondered? As it did not appear that I was going to get a response to my inward question, I just sat silent again. Then Jesus answered my question.

"The embodiment that I am is the same as the Father. It is the same as you. I came down to Earth to show mankind a better way of living; to show mankind a more righteous way to follow the Father's commandments. If you live your life as I have lived mine, then you will come unto the Father. My life is the truth that all of you seek. My relationship to the Father is the relationship you desire. My love for the Father is the only love you need. As I am, therefore can you be."

My mind was reeling with questions. How could I possibly be like Jesus when I was so full of sin? His answer shook me to my core.

"My light cleanses you of all of your imperfections. My very being is like the morning after a night of darkness. In the light of the sun, darkness is forgotten."

The proof of God's love for all of us was right here in front of me. He had, in effect, sent his son down to Earth to remind all of us of whose children we really are. In the simplicity of Jesus' statements to his disciples were the fundamental truths for all of mankind to see.

I was awestruck.

How could I possibly be worthy of sitting here in the shining presence of this great one? His love, his tenderness, his compassion, were so unbelievably strong that I could not have denied Him anything. In fact, I immediately fell weeping at His feet. Those feet which still bore the marks of his crucifixion. As I tenderly placed my lips upon His feet to kiss them, I made a firm commitment to walk only in the Master's shoes, to let his life be the example that I followed in my own commitment to God.

As I laid my face upon his feet, I could hear the angels singing about the blood of the lamb. Then I realized for the first time that the song was not just about blood, but was more importantly about sacrifice. God sacrificed the presence of his son so that his son could manifest a physical presence on Earth. Jesus sacrificed his life so that mankind could be healed of its imperfections.

At this point, I began crying harder, and could hear Jesus assuring me that He understood. In my own mind, I knew that He could deny me nothing. With this thought, I fell into a deep state of prayer and devotion. When I awoke the next morning, my heart was much lighter, and I felt just a tiny bit wiser. I could hardly believe that all of this was happening to me. I kept asking myself what I had done to deserve the honor being given. After much thinking on the subject, I decided that it was God's will, and God's will alone, that was responsible for what was happening to me. The best thing I could do was to pay attention to what my life was trying to show me, in each moment, and to remain devoted to God's presence. Troy had not given me any indication that I would see Jesus again, and for some reason that did not bother me. I just wanted to live a good Baptist life, and to express the love of Jesus in my attitude and behavior.

Three months went by before I saw Troy again. Once again, Mom had just put me and my brother to bed when I heard Troy's voice.

"Get up sleepyhead."

I opened my eyes and found myself floating above my body. I was joyful because I got to go back to the other side. Troy nodded his head in agreement and gathered me in his arms. For the first time in a very long time I found myself in the tunnel of light. I wondered why we were going this way, but knew better than to ask any questions. Soon Troy and I arrived on the astral plane. We stopped in front of the yellow-hued building that I remembered so well. As we went inside, there was an air of nervous excitement. People were rushing towards the same place. Troy guided me along and we stopped in front of a large door. Troy opened the door and we stepped inside a large auditorium. There must have been thousands and thousands of seats, most of which were already filled.

"Troy, what is going on?"

"A very special meeting."

I heard a voice shout my name and looked up to see Ariel waving his arms. He had saved some seats for us, very close to a single chair sitting in the middle of the auditorium. As Troy and I sat down, there was a great air of expectancy.

The crowd became quiet and we all could see a white ball of light descending from the ceiling of the auditorium. It moved very slowly and came to a halt in front of the only empty chair in the room. All of a sudden, there was a cry of recognition and joy. The Master had descended to this plane in order to speak to the citizens of this level. As He began to speak, his voice sounded like the purest harmony one could ever hope to hear. I closed my eyes and began to concentrate on his voice.

"Seek ye first the Kingdom of God, and His righteousness; and all these things shall be added unto you. You are on this level to learn about the lives you have just left. But, I say unto you, did any of you put God first in your lives? Did any of you seek to know my Father in all of his myriad forms?

"You may be asking yourself, where is the Kingdom of God? But, I say unto you, His kingdom is everywhere. It is the child who asked for your help. It is your neighbor who smiled and laughed with you at some kindness or good fortune in your life. It is the beggar who asked you for food. In other words, my children, God's kingdom is all around you, and His kingdom is within each and every one of you."

Jesus paused for a moment. His eyes shining with such

divine love that I just could not look upon them. How could I? I should not have even been there. I just could not get past the fact that I didn't deserved any of what was happening to me. Yet I knew in my heart that if I were to express any of these feelings to Jesus, He would assure me that I was exactly where I was meant to be.

I felt his love surround me and completely fill me. I knew in that moment that the only thing left for me to do was to surrender to God. Surrender to this love that was lifting me to higher levels. No more questions, no more doubt. I had been given the chance to understand a little more about life and the direction my life should be taking, by being granted access to the life beyond death. I made up my mind, right then and there, not to squander any more moments of my life. I would seek God's kingdom first in my life. The only thing I wanted was to know God's love. Having made that decision, I held my head up and gazed into the eyes of pure love. In his eyes, I was dust. In his eyes, I was love. In his eyes, I was devotion. Jesus smiled; I wept. I had never experienced such love as I was experiencing in that moment.

The whole auditorium seemed to be expanding with the power of the Master's love for his Father. Jesus began speaking again.

"Seek ye first the Kingdom of God. There is no greater mission in life than to know my Father. God's love should be first in your lives. When His love is first in your life, then everything you need shall be yours. Notice, I said everything you need, not everything you want. My Father does not always grant your wants because those wants are not always in your best interest. Each one of you should be living a life that is full of wonder and love. Life is a challenge, but it is also an opportunity for growth and harmony. Seeking God first, puts your life in balance. Then God's righteousness, or his right way of living, becomes the focal point in your life. You do not have to do anything. God will do it all for you. Just surrender to His will."

Once again, the Master paused and seemed to go into prayer. As I glanced around, I could see that some people did not know what to do. They did not understand how to put the Master's words into practice.

"Troy," I whispered, "how do we best put the Master's words into practice in our lives."

Troy leaned over to me and said, "Just do it."

It was that simple, and that difficult. But I didn't care. I knew that I was going to try as hard as I could to put God first in my life.

As I once again looked at Jesus sitting in the chair, He seemed to expand. I could actually feel the heat of his body seeming to get closer and closer to me. I closed my eyes and mentally willed myself to accept whatever Jesus was trying to show me. I could feel others in the arena also beginning to accept the words of the Master into their hearts. We sat in prayer and it seemed as if there were not a thousand or so people sitting in prayer, but just one being learning, growing, and becoming all that it could be.

I thought about how on the astral level, one is lovingly guided to look at the life they have just left, and to really see all of the lessons that they had both learned and not learned. If one could look at their life in a honest manner, then one could see how well they had followed the edict of the Master, which is to seek God first. But I thought, there are so many things in life to distract us. How does one go about putting God first so completely in their lives? I wanted to ask Jesus how He was able to accomplish this. But then I remembered that He is the Son of God. Yet somehow I knew that, in our own little way, each of us could live our lives as Jesus did. His life was the best example of surrendering to the will of God.

After I had this thought, I felt as if a great cloud had lifted from my heart. I then began to concentrate on the Master himself trying to experience whatever I needed to experience from Him. I think other people in the crowd were doing the same thing because suddenly the arena exploded into white light. This light was so intense that it burned through me and imprinted itself on my heart. I felt as if I had been marked by the Master as one of his own. Then I heard the sound of wailing. People were crying out the Master's name; calling Him savior and blessed one. I heard myself cry out for God's will to be done here and on Earth. Then I began repeating over and over again: Lord, I surrender. But it wasn't just me repeating those words; other people joined in. Soon I felt a rush of pure light enter and surround me. I felt myself being lifted up, and opened my eyes to see exactly what was happening to me. Jesus was still sitting down in the chair, but all of us were being lifted into the air. It was such an incredible feeling of love and joy. People were both laughing and crying. The joy that permeated all of us was so infectious that no one was left untouched.

I felt a hand on my shoulder and Troy said to me, "It is almost time for me to return you to Earth."

I absolutely did not want to go.

"Troy, is the lecture over?"

"No, this will go on for a long time. Jesus is giving all of us here exactly what we need to help us grow."

Suddenly I got it. Whether or not it was really time for me to be returned to Earth was irrelevant. I had already gotten exactly what I needed from this event.

"Okay, Troy, I am ready to go."

Troy looked at me in amazement.

"How can you, a mere child, understand so quickly, what it sometimes takes other people years to get?"

"Because I am a child, Troy, I am open to all of life's experiences. I have not yet learned to shut myself down as most adults do. Hopefully, I never will."

Troy smiled at me, and said, "You are truly a Little One."

"Troy, as long as I live I will not forget these experiences that I am having on the other side of life. I will always try to surrender to the will of God. That's all I can or should do."

Troy once again shook his head in amazement.

"I am beginning to understand why you have been granted these experiences. Someday I hope I will understand everything about you."

"Why wouldn't you, big brother?"

He did not answer, but instead picked me up. As we turned to go, I once again glanced at Jesus. He was still seated on the chair. Yet, I knew that He was not really on the chair, He was everywhere. He opened his eyes and his gaze penetrated me to the core. In my mind, I heard Him say to me, "Where I am, there may ye be also. It is all up to you."

Yes it is, I thought, and I am going to try to follow you, my Lord, to the best of my ability.

With that thought in mind, and the blessing of the Master upon my heart, Troy returned me to my body on Earth. After he settled me into my body, rather than leaving right away, he just stood at the foot of my bed and stared at me.

"What's wrong, Troy?"

At first he didn't answer, but then he said to me, "You were vibrating at a very high rate as I carried you back to the Earth level. Even now I can see you vibrating. It is as if I brought back a different being."

"No, Troy, you brought back a child who has a clearer understanding of her life. I may continue to make mistakes, but I will always try to surrender myself, in each moment, to God the Father."

My answer must have satisfied him because he just smiled at me and vanished. I thought about what I had seen and heard for a long time before I finally fell asleep.

The next day, the memory of my encounter with Jesus helped me to remain in the light of the Master all day long.

My mother noticed that I was a little withdrawn and asked me, "Is something wrong?"

"No, I'm just thinking about what I learned last night."

She didn't try to get me to talk more. She always seemed to know when I needed to work something out in my own mind.

Nap time came faster than normal that day; and as I laid down in my bed, I felt the warmth of my mother's love surround me. After she left the room, I began to feel myself rise up and away from my body.

"Hello sis," said Troy.

"Hi Troy."

He then informed me that he was going to take me back to the astral level because of a number of questions that I wanted to ask him. I didn't bother to ask him how he knew, I just nodded my head in agreement.

Soon, I was again standing in front of the door to Ariel's classroom. Ariel turned as I entered the room, and greeted me with a hug. As I took my seat, I noticed that there were a few other people entering the room also. Each one was given a hug by Ariel. After we had all taken our seats, Ariel began to speak.

"All of you have been brought back here to my classroom because of the questions you have regarding the appearance of the Master here on this level. Let me begin by saying that the Master often journeys to this level to speak to people like you. It is a measure of the love that He has for mankind that causes Him to return here. Someday you will be able to join the Master on his level."

Many people immediately shook their heads no.

Ariel was quite stern in his response, "Did none of you even listen to the Master's words? He told you where His Father's kingdom is. He even told you how to enter that kingdom. If it were meant for Jesus alone to be in the Kingdom of God, then He would not be descending to this level to help you understand that where He is, there should you be also."

Ariel paused. The stillness seemed to create a space of perfect understanding. Suddenly, a woman began to laugh. Then the rest of us joined in. It was as if something had been released and we were now free to be the children of God that the Master had urged us to be.

I raised my hand to ask Ariel a question, "Ariel, can we ask Jesus questions?"

Ariel smiled at me and replied, "Yes."

Someone in the room then exclaimed, "I would be too afraid to ask Jesus any questions."

"Why?" asked Ariel.

"Because," the person replied, "I am too insignificant."

I leaned over to Troy and asked him, "What does insignificant mean?"

"Someone, or something, that has very little meaning to anyone or anything."

"How can someone think that, Troy?"

"Easy! How did you feel when you first saw Jesus?"

"I felt totally unworthy."

"That is a part of feeling insignificant."

"Oh."

Ariel answered the person by asking him, "Do you feel that an ant is insignificant to God?"

"Oh, no," the man replied.

"Then," Ariel responded, "how can you possibly feel insignificant?"

I could see a light dawning on the man's face, "You are right, Ariel, nothing is insignificant to God."

I could see that the other people in the room had also understood the meaning of Ariel's conversation with this man.

"When you are ready, each of you will have the opportunity to ask Jesus any question your heart desires," said Ariel.

One lady then asked Ariel, "What is the best way to be around the Master? And if you want to ask Him questions, what is the best way to go about doing that?"

"Go to Him with only love in your heart. By doing this, you will naturally know how to be around Him. Any question you ask of Him should be sincere, and should come from a space of truly wanting to know the answer."

With that response, everyone seemed satisfied.

Ariel signaled that the class was over. He had not convened the class to answer our questions himself, but rather to assure us that we could ask the Master any questions directly, when we were ready. Everyone in the room seemed very excited.

As each person left the room, Ariel whispered something into their ear. Whatever he was saying to them, caused them a great deal of happiness. As I stood to leave, Ariel came to me and whispered that soon I would be able to ask the Master my question or questions. I thanked him.

Troy then gathered me in his arms and soon I found myself floating above my body. I wanted to ask Troy when I would see Jesus again. Instead, I decided that I would just be patient. Besides, I wasn't really sure what particular question I wanted to ask the Master, even though Ariel seemed to know my question already.

Troy acknowledged my confusion and said, "I will return when you are ready."

I didn't really understand why I was so reluctant to see Jesus again. I suppose, if I had not wanted to ask Him a question, it would have been very easy to just sit near Him and gaze into his eyes.

"Troy, don't forget to come and get me when I am ready."

"Don't worry, I won't forget."

With those words ringing in my ears, I quickly fell asleep.

Six months went by before I again heard my brother's voice.

"How are you, Kathie?"

"I'm fine."

I was trying not to get excited, but I knew that if Troy were here, it could only be for one reason.

"Are you ready?" asked Troy.

I thought about that question for a moment and then replied, "Yes."

This time it felt as if I were slowly floating out of my body, as if I really did not want to leave it. I glanced at Troy and he was smiling.

"Do you still feel that you are unworthy of all of these adventures?"

"I sure do! But, there must be a good reason for all of these things happening to me. I have decided to just let all of this happen and think about it later."

Troy laughed and picked me up. The transition was almost instantaneous. One moment I was in my bedroom and the next, I was on a level where I could sit with the Master. Once again I stood in front of the building that seemed to be glowing with love. As I glanced around, I saw Ariel and Aurora coming to join us. I greeted both of them with a shout of joy. Both of them gave me hugs in greeting.

"What are you two doing here?" I asked.

Both of them laughed, and Aurora responded by saying, "Anytime we can sit with the Master, we waste no time in doing so."

"Are you two my guardian angels?" I asked.

A look of joy passed between the both of them and they responded in unison, "yes." They once again hugged me and we went inside the building and into the room where I had first seen Jesus. This time He was already in the room and motioned for all of us to be seated. I sat as far away as I could. I could not look Him straight in the eyes. I kept my head down, trying to avoid being noticed by Him, and closed my eyes.

Being in his presence was like standing in a fountain of the holiest and purest love. It was as if He could see no wrong in me or anyone else for that matter. I noticed that no one was talking. In a room of about twenty people, no one was talking. I opened my eyes just to see what was going on, and found myself staring into His eyes only a few inches from mine. My eyes widened in surprise and I started laughing. I couldn't help myself. I just started laughing because I was filled with such joy that it bubbled up and spilled out of me as laughter. Soon everyone in the room was laughing, including Jesus himself.

"That's better!" said Jesus.

I stopped laughing and began to smile. For the first time since all of this had begun, I truly felt that this indeed was where I belonged.

As Jesus returned to his seat, He asked, "Does anyone in the room have any questions?"

My hand shot up immediately. I was no longer shy. Somehow I knew that if I wanted to ask Him a question, this was the moment to do so.

"Jesus," I asked, "could you please tell me how to live a better life on Earth so that when my physical body is no more, I can return to this level and be with you for eternity?"

"Only with me, Little One?"

I thought about that for a moment and then said, "Well, actually, I want to be with you and your Father. Will that ever be possible, Master?"

His smile was like a burst of sunlight on a dark and stormy day.

"My child, all things are possible with my Father."

With those words spoken from his own mouth, I began to cry. Troy rushed over to me.

"Kathie, are you okay?"

"Yes, Troy. There is nothing wrong. I am just so happy that I can hardly contain it. My heart wants to sing and cry at the same time."

Both Ariel and Aurora then gave me a hug and offered words of encouragement.

I looked at Jesus, and asked Him, "Can I come over to you and sit at your feet?"

He nodded his head yes, and I raced over to His side. As I sat at his feet, I could see the actual holes from His terrible ordeal on the cross. A part of me wanted to touch His holy feet, but felt that to do so would be sacrilegious.

"No, my child. If I could allow Thomas to touch them, why wouldn't I allow you, who loves me so much?"

Once again I began crying. I just could not understand what I had done in my short little life, to deserve to be sitting at the feet of my Master.

I heard Him say, "Do not question God's will, Little One. Just enjoy what He has given to you this day."

Upon hearing those words, I placed my hands on the feet of my most beloved Master. Immediately I felt myself rising, as a bolt of energy shot through me. Suddenly, I felt another bolt of energy upon my head as Jesus touched the top of my head, to keep me from rising off the floor. I clung to his feet as if my very soul depended upon my doing so. His voice, so pure and so soft, filled the room.

"She is so open to me. Her love is so complete that this is her moment of full surrender."

His words filled me with such Divine Love that, in my heart, I knew that what He had just said was the absolute truth. My heart began to sing a song of utter and complete surrender to Him. The touch of my hands on His feet, and His hand on my head, was the key to the opening of my heart. For a long while, I knew no more, as I bathed in the radiance of His magnificent love for me and for all of mankind.

I sat with Him like that for a little while, before I again

heard His voice. My heart was so full of joy that I knew from this moment on I would fear no evil, for my heart and my soul belonged to Him. As He began to answer my question, I marveled at His wisdom and His gentleness.

"Blessed are the pure in heart, for they shall see God." He bent His head down towards me, and said, "Kathie, you wanted to know how you can live a better life on the Earth level. Be pure in heart. By pure in heart, I mean, live your life in a manner that is pleasing to my Father. You can do so, by putting God first in your life. Each moment of your life can teach you something about yourself. Learn more. Grow more. When you are challenged by what life is offering you, dedicate that moment to God. Offer up the prayer, thy will not mine be done. At the time of my darkest moment, in the Garden of Gethsemane, the light began to show through when I realized and accepted that my Father's will must be done in my life. Even though I knew that I would be hung on a cross, and that I would lose my life in a very painful and horrible way, it was all the will of my Father. How could I deny my Father anything? I did what He wanted me to do, for the good of all mankind."

He paused for a moment, and I asked Him this question, "My beloved Master, how did you know what was God's will?"

Jesus smiled and said, "Because, it was not my will to die in such a despicable manner. I would have much preferred a more quiet death."

I thought about what He was trying to tell me. His heart was made pure, because He had accepted God's will for Him. All of his life, He had prayed to know what God wanted Him to do with his life; and once He knew, He did just what God wanted him to. His purity of will had made His heart pure;

and in His darkest hour, He had seen His Father, and had made the ultimate sacrifice.

Jesus again repeated, "Blessed are the pure in Heart, for they shall see God. A child comes into the world open and with a pure heart. Depending upon the circumstances of his upbringing, his heart may remain pure or he may become sullied by the world as he enters adulthood. To remain pure in heart is to remain pure in spirit. Kathie, your life is just beginning. Seek God first. Strive to know His will for you, and you will forever be strong in His sight. Everyday, you should ask yourself, is what I am about to do my will or God's will? Listen for God's voice. He will show you the way. Dedicate your every waking moment to my Father, and be about His business only. For surely, He will take care of you as He does all of his creatures."

"Where is God's voice?" I asked Jesus.

He placed his hand on the area of my heart, and gently said, "Right here. *It will be as a still small voice within you.* Listen for it. Set aside each day some time, to be still and to listen. My Father's voice is like the quiet of a snowflake falling onto the ground; and yet, it is also like the roar of a mighty wave on the ocean. If you listen, you will hear Him."

Jesus stopped talking, and all of us sat in the silence. As I clung to his feet and concentrated on his words, I began to hear a voice deep within me. Very quiet at first, and then louder and louder. All is Love. All is Love. All is Love. All is Love. All is Love. All is Love. All is Love. Those three words began to consume me. My Heart began to sing; and suddenly, I was surrounded by a light so pure it had no color. It uplifted me, and then I knew and understood the oh so precious words of Jesus. I was seeing really clearly for the first time in my life. I knew in my heart that I had always belonged to God, and that

I had no other choice but to try to understand and do the will of He who had made me, indeed He who had made us all.

Although, I had thought that the answer I would get from Jesus would be long, complicated, and difficult to understand, I should have known better. He had given me a simple and understandable way to live my life; and whatever happened to me, I knew that I would try to live my life in the manner that had been given to me by Him. I sat with him for a long time that night, listening to His holy words, and trying to understand all that He was saying to us. When He was done speaking, all of us in the room quietly sat with the Master, in order for His words to expand into our very souls. During that time, I never once let go of His feet. I felt as if I were being infused with the Masters Love and Grace.

All too soon, it was time for me to return to the Earth level. This time, however, I did not protest my going. I did, however, have just one more question for Jesus.

"Master, will I ever see you again?"

His smile was like a thousand suns beaming down on me.

"Yes, Little One, you will see me again, and not just here on this level. Look for me in all things, and surely you will see me."

I stood up and gave Him the biggest smile I could. Then, I bowed before him, and thanked him for His kind words. He placed His hand upon my head, in a gesture of parting, and then was gone from my sight. I could not talk, and just began to cry.

Ariel gathered me up in his arms, motioned for Troy and Aurora to leave us, and Ariel returned me to my body, sleeping on my bed.

As Ariel lowered me into my body, he said, "You will remember all that has been said tonight; and if you follow the words of the Master, then you will indeed be doing God's will."

"Thank you, Ariel, for all of your guidance and help."

"Don't worry, Little One, these visits are not over. On the contrary, they are just beginning."

I smiled, and thanked God for His kindness and love, in allowing me to have all of these experiences.

"I will not forget," I declared to Ariel, and anyone else listening. "I will remember always."

The next morning, I awoke with a new sense of purpose, and a new comittment to live my life in a more positive and spiritual manner.

The words of the Master became a tapestry for my life. To be pure in heart was to live my life for and about God. His will, and His will alone, became the words that I spoke to myself.

As I sat up to get out of my bed, I saw my mother sitting beside me.

"Hi Mom. You will not believe who I spent the night with, and what I learned from Him."

"Kathie, I know who you spoke to last night. Because early this morning, I came in here to check on you, and I could not believe what I saw. Your body was glowing with a white light, and you had an angelic look on your face. As a matter of fact, you were smiling and crying, both at the same time. But, I knew that you were okay, because your whole being radiated divine love."

My mind was blown, but my heart felt so pure. I tried to get her to explain to me, a little more of what she had seen or felt, but she was unable to do so.

9

Epilogue: Reunion

Many years after my series of adventures with Troy, I again began to see him. These events occured after my mother had announced that during a routine chest X-ray the doctors had found a small spot on her lungs. A biopsy was performed and we were told that the spot was malignant. But they had taken it all out and it had not spread to any other tissue. The doctors wanted to do some radiation therapy and felt that there would be no additional problems. She was pretty upbeat about the situation, but I could tell that she was a little scared. I noticed that she had begun seeing Troy again.

As we sat talking one day, she asked me, "Have you seen Troy recently?"

"Yes, but not in the same way that I used to see him when I was a child."

"Well, I see him around me all the time."

I felt a strong sense of foreboding. From what I remembered from my various classes on the other side, sometimes when a person's time is short on Earth, relatives who had already passed on will often hang around the person to help prepare him or her for the great transition.

I guess my mother must have sensed my apprehension because she immediately said to me, "Troy has not given me any indication that my time has come. Besides, I am just not ready to go yet."

I breathed a sigh of relief. Although I knew that her time was indeed limited, I put a smile on my face and we began to talk about other things.

Later that evening, Troy came and pulled me out of my body. Once again, we raced through the tunnel of light and soon stood in front of the yellow-hued building that I remembered so well.

"Troy, why are we here? It has been ages since I sat in one of these classrooms."

"This is a special class to teach you how to deal with grief."

His words chilled me to the bone.

"Don't worry, Kathie. You are not going to lose her soon. But her earthly life will be coming to an end in a few years."

After speaking those words, Troy led me into one of the many classrooms. As I looked around the room, I noticed that this room was indeed very small. Imagine my surprise when Ariel walked into the room.

"Ariel," I cried, "it is so good to see you!"

Ariel gave me the biggest hug and smiled deeply into my face.

"Ariel," I said, "why am I here?"

He smiled and said, "A few people in your situation will be joining us tonight."

"In my situation?"

Ariel gave me a look of pure sympathy.

"Ariel, what is the topic of this class?"

"Learning to let go."

As I thought about Ariel's last words, the other students arrived, and a nice calm descended on the classroom.

Ariel began by saying, "All of you are facing a situation where by the time it ends, you will have to let go of someone who is very near and dear to you."

All of us sat up straighter and glanced at one another.

"You are in the process of losing one or both of your parents. That is one of the great challenges on Earth. People find it hard to let go of relatives. Death seems so final and they just cannot bear the thought of not ever seeing their beloved relative again."

I could tell that Ariel's words were having an effect on all of us. I thought about my mother and the great adventure that awaited her. Since there was so much to see and do on this side of life, I felt selfish wanting her to stay with me any longer than she had to. Yet I was just not ready to say goodbye; even though I knew that I would have to someday.

Ariel let his words sink-in before he continued. "The topic of this class is: learning to let go of your loved one, as a part of the 'dying' experience. What you have to remember is that the separation you will feel when your loved one leaves is, in the scheme of things, for a very short time. Now, let me explain how to let go.

"The first thing you must do is to keep the lines of communication open between you and your loved one. Don't stop communicating! People who are going through the dying process should be allowed to express how they are feeling. Too often people do not want to hear anyone talk about their upcoming death. It reminds them too much of their own mortality—an issue that oftentimes people are not quite ready to face. It is very difficult to imagine life going on without your loved one, or your own life ending."

"So, what do you do when someone comes to you and tells you that they have a terminal illness? Do you run away by turning off your ears? Do you retreat to some fantasy world where death does not exist? Do you start grieving immediately from the unbearable pain of the upcoming separation? Or, do you listen with an open heart and an open mind?"

"Listening to someone tell you that they are dying, or even worse, listening to some doctor tell you that your loved one only has a limited time left on Earth, is one of the worst experiences you will have to endure. At that point, you will begin grieving. But, that is the worst thing you could do. It is at this time in life that you will need to remain by the side of your loved one and be strong. Throughout the time that you have remaining, remember that you will see your loved one again. Death is not the end, it is only the beginning of another life. Another chance to grow and be all that you can be."

Somehow, Ariel's words brought me much comfort. I could tell that his words were having the same effect on the other students in the class.

"Now, don't get me wrong. This will be a difficult experience for you. But it will be much easier if you can keep in mind what I am talking to you about."

"Ariel," I asked, "how can we help to keep people's spirits up when there is so much sadness around?"

"Each moment that you live on the earthly plane can teach you what you need to learn about life. Even death can teach you about life. How you respond in the face of death will either hurt or help your loved one. You must be as supportive as you can be. One of the key words here is that you must listen to everything that is going on around you. Let your mother or father talk to you about any and everything, including any funeral plans or disposition of their earthly goods. Always bear in mind that they will need you to be honest about your feelings. Communication and the willingness to listen to what is such a painful subject for most people, is what is required."

"But Ariel," I said, "grieving is such a natural part of life. Perhaps, what is missing for some people during this time, is the ability to cry together."

"Yes, you have to remember that the person who is dying also has to learn to let go. They have their own grieving process to go through. Being able to sit with someone and hold them, to calm both of your fears, will in the long run be very beneficial to all concerned."

Ariel then asked, "What part of the dying process do people fear the most?"

I thought about his question for a moment, then responded by saying, "Leaving their loved ones behind."

Someone else said, "The pain associated with the dying process."

Another one said, "The thought of life on Earth continuing without you. Few can imagine life going on without them in it."

Ariel smiled and said, "All three answers are correct. But the greatest fear of all is the thought of nothingness. Death is the great unknown and people usually fear the unknown.

But in actuality, what you see as death, we see as birth. While you are dying to the earthly plane, you are being born onto this level. Just as, so long ago, you were born onto the earthly plane, as you died to this level. Death is the reversal of how you arrived onto the earthly plane.

Now, some of you may still be wondering about how to let go, even with the knowledge you now have about what happens after the body is still. Look for the signs that are all around you. Give your loved one all of the support and love needed. At the appointed time, if you are with your dying relative, be sure to tell them that it is okay for them to let go of their body, then wish them a safe and speedy journey. By doing so you will be letting go in a positive manner."

With these words, Ariel indicated, with a nod of his head that the class was over. I sat in my seat for a few moments, reflecting on what he had said. I think all of us in the room knew that our upcoming task would not be an easy one. But we knew in our hearts that we would do the very best that we could.

As I walked towards Ariel, he turned to me and said, "Your road ahead will be difficult. But with all of the lessons you have learned, you will be able to persevere."

"Thank you, Ariel. This class has helped me a great deal."

With those words spoken, I gave Ariel a hug and indicated to Troy that I was ready to leave.

The next morning I woke up with a new resolve in my life. I didn't know how much time I had left with my mother but I was going to make sure that the time we had left together would be meaningful and full of love.

Thus began a period of listening to my mother describe how she was feeling. Her moments of pain and discomfort were eased by being able to talk to me about what she was going through, including her fear of dying. She told me that she did not want to die and leave everyone behind.

"Mom, have you been seeing Troy around?" I asked.

She smiled and said to me, "Yes, I have."

"What does that mean, Mom?"

She thought for a moment, then smiled and said, "It means that someday I will see all of you again."

"Yes, our separation will only be for a relatively short time. Just think, Mom, you will see for yourself all of the things that I have been telling you about for all of these years and you will once again get to see your mother and father."

It was as if a light bulb had been turned on in her head. She then smiled and gave me the biggest hug. The sadness had disappeared from her room. I then brought in the dozen roses I had bought for her.

"What's this?" she asked. "They're beautiful!"

I laughed and said, "I want to give you flowers now. I don't want to wait until it is too late for you to see the flowers with your earthly eyes."

"Makes sense."

We then went on to talk about how she wanted her personal items distributed, a conversation made much easier because Troy had taken me to see Ariel.

It would be three long years before Mom would succumb to cancer. Two years before that, I decided to go to India with a few friends. Mom was concerned about me being so far away, and we almost had a minor fight about it. But after she saw that I was determined to go, she acquiesced. I asked her if she wanted me to bring her anything. She mentioned that she would like to have a cashmere shawl, like the one I often wore when I visited her.

I was in India for five weeks. Although, on the whole, it was a wonderful experience, I couldn't wait to get home to see my mother and tell her about all of my adventures in

India. I returned the day before Christmas, and I went to see her. She looked as well as could be expected.

She took me back into her bedroom and said, "I'm so happy to have you back. I didn't have anyone to talk to about what I am going through. No one wanted to hear me talk about funeral plans or anything else having to do with death."

I smiled and said, "I will not be going anyplace else for a long time."

Somehow, all of the family realized this would be her last Christmas on this Earth. So we made it as special as we could, without being too depressing. It was a warm and lovely holiday, with lots of family stories and joy that we were all together for what may be our last time. In spite of her illness, my mom looked radiant and cooked one of her best Christmas dinners ever. Later on, as I left her house for the evening, I gave thanks for the happy memories I would always have of this day.

During the early part of 1979, Mom's health slowly declined as the cancer spread to other parts of her body. Still, she remained as upbeat as she could for the sake of her family. During that time she began to see Troy more and more. Of course, no one else in the family believed her. But I knew, and was happy that her beloved son was now taking care of the spirit of this woman who had been our mother in this life.

The Thanksgiving holiday would be the test of all that I had been taught in my last class with Ariel. The Wednesday night before Thanksgiving, I was up late doing all of the preparation that I could do for the dinner we were having the next day. I wanted it to be perfect because I had invited Mom and Dad over, and surprisingly Mom had agreed to come. This surprised me because I knew that she was in a great deal of pain. But she indicated to me Wednesday night that she was feeling much better.

When I awakened Thanksgiving morning, I wasn't feeling well myself. I took my temperature and was surprised to learn that it had risen overnight to 104 degrees. I called my mom to find out if she was really going to come over. She sounded healthy and strong and assured me that she would be coming over. I dragged myself out of bed and began to prepare dinner. While the turkey was cooking, I returned to bed to rest. Even though my temperature was high, I knew that I was having a malarial attack and that it would not last longer than 48 hours. Still, I was very miserable, and felt weak. When dinner was ready, I phoned my parents.

My dad answered the phone and said, "I don't think that your mom is really up to coming over for dinner."

"Daddy, I'm sick also, but I really want both of you to come over. If you can't eat, at least sit with me. I'll prepare a couple of plates to send back with you. That way, you can eat when you feel like it."

"Okay, I'll ask your mother, and call you back with her answer."

I didn't understand my response at first. But realized that I felt a sense of urgency about the situation, as if I knew that I would never again be able to cook a Thanksgiving dinner for my parents together. The phone rang. They were coming, but wanted it understood that they would only be able to stay for a little while. I rushed around my apartment and got everything ready.

When they arrived, my dad had to help my mother walk. I knew right then and there that he was right, she should have stayed home.

As she walked through my door, the first thing she said to me was, "You should be in bed."

She touched my forehead and could not believe that I had managed to cook dinner with such a high fever. As I put the food on the table, all of us sat down to eat except my mom. She really was not hungry.

"I made the dressing exactly as you taught me," I said to her.

She then asked for a little bit of it, and managed to clean her plate.

My dad smiled, and said to me, "This is the first bit of food she has eaten in a few days."

All too soon my mother said, "It is time for us to return home. You should go right to bed as soon as we leave."

She was so much sicker than I was. Yet she was able to mother me for what would be the last time. She even tucked me into bed, the same way she had done it when I was a little girl.

By then, my fever had risen dangerously high. I guess she knew how sick I really was. I waved goodbye to her, as she left my room.

Later on in the evening she called to check on me. As I groggily answered the phone, I assured her that my fever had gone down a little bit and that I was going to be okay. She then thanked me for the lovely dinner I had prepared and assured me that she had eaten some more once she had returned home.

"Okay, Mom. I love you, and thanks for coming over, even though you were sick."

"I love you too, Kathie."

Christmas 1979 was a huge family affair. Even though we had thought that the previous Christmas would be her last, Mom once again, to my complete joy, had proven all of us wrong. However, there could be no denying that she was indeed sicker this Christmas than the last one. Therefore, all of us made sure that her day was a happy one. As I left the house that year, I could not help but wonder what Christmas 1980 would be like.

"Don't worry about the future," I heard Troy say. "Just enjoy this moment, for this is all you have."

As I thought about what he had said to me, I realized that no matter what happened in the upcoming year, at this moment in time my mother was with me in her earthly body. Let the future take care of itself.

Mom had several problems during the early part of 1980. Her health went up and down. She rarely left her bed and our talks became more serious as she indicated to me what she wanted done with some of her possessions. These talks always included her visits with Troy. She said that Troy was trying to ease her mind about her upcoming transition. Sometimes these talks would become unbearable for me. But I always tried to remember what Ariel had said about open communication, and would listen patiently while she described what she was seeing. I continued bringing her flowers. It became our special silent joke.

By the time November arrived, it had become painfully obvious to all of us that Mom's condition was rapidly deteriorating. The week before Thanksgiving 1980, my dad took her to the hospital. At first, she seemed to be making progress. She stopped talking about seeing Troy. It was as if she really was trying to stay here with all of us. She even talked about going home again. These visits were oftentimes filled with stories about her own mom and dad. It was as if she were going back in time.

During the first week of December, she began to talk about seeing birds, flowers, and colors in her room. Some of her family members begged her not to talk like that and felt that she was hallucinating. I, however, knew better. When we were alone together, I would try to encourage her to be open with me, and tell me everything she was seeing. It was amazing to me how clearly she could see the next level. Also, I was surprised to see how many astral beings were arriving at her room, surrounding my mother with so much love that I knew her journey would be a safe one. During that time period, Mom was clearly present on this level. Though, she was constantly talking about the astral beings she was seeing, she was still very coherent.

During one visit, the nurse came into the room and asked me to leave for a few minutes so she could perform a certain medical procedure. She pulled the curtain around my mother and all of a sudden I heard a sharp squeal that almost sounded like a cat. I was trying to place the sound when I realized that the sound was coming from my mother. Apparently she didn't like what was being done to her, and neither did I, for that matter. After the nurse had finished, I went back into the room. Mom was quiet.

"Does the indignity of being in the hospital bother you?" I asked her.

She slowly nodded her head yes, and began to cry. It felt as if someone had ripped the heart from my body to see this strong woman so helpless. I gave her a big hug and told her how much I loved her. As I sat next to her holding her hand, I saw Troy standing at the end of her bed.

"Mom," I asked, "can you see who is standing at the end of your bed?"

She looked up for a moment and began to smile. Her son was here to help her.

"I need to spend some time alone with her, to prepare

her for her upcoming experience. I want to assure her that she will not be going through this alone," said Troy.

As I turned to leave, I said to my mom, "I will return on Sunday."

She nodded her head and then suddenly said, in a loud, strong and clear voice, "I love you, Kathie."

I smiled back at her and said, "I love you, too."

Sunday arrived. As I prepared to go to the hospital, I thought about her upcoming birthday on Tuesday. I knew that all of the family was going to be there, as we wanted to make this birthday a most special one. When I walked into her room, the first thing I noticed was the feeding tube in her nose. I thought to myself, I know you don't like that experience, Mom. As I said hello to her, she barely acknowledged me.

Then, all of a sudden, she looked at me and asked this most surprising question, "Who are all of those 'niggers' around you?"

I looked at her in complete surprise.

"What niggers?"

She looked at me again, and said, "The niggers standing around you."

Now I was completely intrigued.

I approached her more closely and asked her, "What do the people you are seeing around me look like?"

"Like black niggers."

I just had to laugh. As I stopped laughing, even Mom seemed very amused. I knew that there were astral beings around me. What mom did not know was that they were Hindus — Indian people. They had been around me since I had gone to India. To Mom, they looked like black people with straight hair. I knew then that this visit would be most interesting. I hoped that the rest of the family would not arrive soon, so that she could be allowed to express to me what she was seeing.

As I sat next to her and held her hand, she suddenly cried out, "Mommy."

I glanced over to where her eyes were looking and saw my grandmother. She was young looking so my mother could remember her at the time of her death. I knew then that she had come to take her daughter home. It seemed strange to hear my own mother crying out to her mother. Mom had come full circle, and was once again a child.

A knock on the door told me that the rest of the family had arrived. They, too, were disturbed by the feeding tube in my mother's nose. But that didn't disturb them nearly as much as my mom telling them about the birds in the corner of the room and the brand new colors she was seeing. Some of my family members tried to discourage her from speaking about what she was seeing. One even told my mother that she was hallucinating and to stop talking about such nonsense. Mom just laughed and continued on. Everything she was seeing I could see, and told everyone at the risk of being ridiculed. I didn't want my mother to think that she was losing her mind.

I stayed with Mom for many hours on that last Sunday of her life. Everyone else had left except my dad. I wanted to stay longer, but knew that Dad needed some time alone with her. I leaned over to her and once again told her how much I loved her, and if she wanted to leave now, she could. I knew that her body was tired, and that her spirit wanted to be free. I told her to have a safe journey, even though I fully expected to see her on her birthday. I just wanted to let her know that I wished her Godspeed on her journey ahead.

Troy smiled and said, "Don't worry! I am going to be taking care of her now."

"Thank you for everything. Please take good care of our mother until she and I meet again," I told him.

As I turned to leave the room, my dad was holding my mom very tenderly. It was somthing I would remember for many years.

"I will return on Tuesday to spend your birthday with you," I said.

On Monday, I called my mom at the hospital. A relative answered the phone and put the receiver to my mom's ear. Her voice sounded very faint as she said hello. It already seemed as if she were looking into eternity.

"Mom," I said, "I love you very much."

Once again, I heard her familiar voice saying, "I love you too, Kathie."

"I will see you tomorrow to help you celebrate your birthday."

"Okay, and goodnight," she said.

The following day, all of us made plans to join her in her hospital room to celebrate what we were sure would be her last birthday. At about 1:30 p.m. I called my brother, Lee, to find out what time he was planning to go to the hospital. We talked on the phone for almost 30 minutes. Then we said our goodbyes and hung up. A few minutes later I felt someone standing near me. I looked up and saw my mother's face. She seemed very happy, and I saw that Troy was with her.

"I came to say goodbye," she said. "I am finally free of that heavy old body."

I was shocked. Troy came and stood next to me.

"It is not yet time for you to go. So, you must say goodbye to our mother for now," Troy whispered into my ear.

"Goodbye for now, Mom," I said.

"I love you," I heard her say, as she faded away.

My mom was gone. She was now in the tunnel of light, in the arms of her beloved son, just as I had done so many times before.

I was barely able to continue working. At the end of the workday, I went to the hospital, just in case my dad or brother had gone there. I went up to my mother's room, and noticed that her bed was indeed empty.

"Where is my mother?" I asked a passing nurse.

"Your mom passed away at exactly two p.m."

"Was my family informed?"

"Yes."

I thanked her and turned to walk away. I glanced back at the bed that had held my mom for a month. The room was quiet, waiting for the next patient to arrive. As I walked out of the hospital, I began crying. She was really gone. For the first time in my life, I would not be able to call her on the phone and tell her my latest problem or joy.

I knew that my family would be worried about me driving in rush hour traffic, having just learned that my mother had passed away. So, I made sure that I concentrated on my driving.

When I arrived at the home of my parents, Dad greeted me at the door with a big hug. Everyone in the room breathed a big sigh of relief. Then we began sharing our favorite stories about the life of my mother. We all cried together as we remembered this very special woman.

As I walked into the kitchen, I heard Troy say, "She is okay, and is sleeping."

I smiled.

"How long will she be asleep, Troy?"

"Only for a few days. I don't want her awake while her funeral is being planned."

"Was she happy to see her relatives?"

Troy laughed and said, "Well, she didn't get to see them for very long, as I wanted her to get some rest."

"What happens now, Troy?"

"You let go, and go on living."

I just could not imagine life without her.

"Oh, don't worry. In a few days you will see her again."

That brought a smile to my face, and lightened my heart a little.

We planned her funeral for Monday, December 22, 1980.

Just as Troy had promised, Mom slept for a few days, and then I was allowed to visit her on the astral level. On Friday, Troy came and got me. He took me directly to her house, which reminded me so much of her earthly home. As I walked through the door, Mom gave a shout and ran to me. She gave me a big hug and told me, over and over again, how much she loved me. She then began introducing me to relatives that I had heard about but never met.

After several of these introductions, Mom took me aside, and asked, "How is your father doing?"

"You know, Mom. He is doing okay. He misses you terribly. But, he will be alright."

"I miss him, too. As wonderful as all of this is, I do miss my family."

"Mom, now you are with your other family, from so long ago."

"Yes, I know. There will be a major party after my earthly funeral and more of my old friends and family will be in attendance."

"Mom, can I come and bring Dad?"

She thought that that was a good idea, and we agreed to meet again that Monday night. Troy then came into the room and reminded my mom that it was time for me to return to my body. As we reluctantly parted, Troy reminded me that I would see her again soon.

The weekend before the funeral, Troy came to me and gave me continuous reports on the well-being of my mother. Still, it just did not seem the same. I could not call her on the phone, but I could get out of my body and go visit her whenever I wanted to. How strange that seemed.

As we went about making funeral arrangements, I wondered if my mother was going to be allowed to come to her funeral. But Troy had disappeared and was not available for me to ask him this important question. I spent most of the weekend with my father and brother, Lee. Once again, we told stories of our experiences with mother and hoped that wherever she was, all was okay with her. Even though we didn't discuss the funeral, it was an ever-present thought on our minds.

Monday, December 22, 1980, dawned bright and early. As I got dressed for the funeral, I couldn't help but wonder what this day was going to bring. As I drove over to my dad's house, I steadied myself for the ordeal ahead.

The limousines arrived on time and the family got into the cars to be driven to Mom's funeral. The church looked beautiful. We all sat down and the service began. Some of my mom's favorite hymns were sung by the soloist. I felt myself about to burst into tears, when I heard a familiar voice. I looked up into the choir stand and there waving to me and the family was my mother. I noticed that Troy was with her, as well as some other astral beings whom I didn't recognize at that point. She seemed very happy. I was pleased that she had been allowed to come to her funeral. It was clear that she was having a good time, all things considered. At the sight of my mother, I didn't know whether to laugh or to cry. Some of my family members were clearly quite distraught and I could sense my mother's sadness at their pain. Several times during the service I saw my mother holding my dad, trying to ease his pain. She kept whispering into his ear how much she loved him and that she would see him again. She went to every person there, and gave them a slight kiss on the cheek. Then she came and stood in front of me. She gave me a big hug and thanked me for telling her my stories so many years ago. It had made her departure so much easier. She then returned to the choir stand and stood next to Troy for the rest of the service. Her face ranged from complete joy and peace to sadness at having to leave us all behind.

As the service concluded, and everyone paraded past her open casket, Mom began jumping up and down and laughing at the expressions of sorrow on the faces of some of the mourners. Then she yelled to me that she wished everyone could see her and know that she was still alive. That is why she was so happy. She knew that someday she would see all of these people again.

After the burial, we gathered at my dad's house. Many of the people brought food, and everyone had a special story to tell about my mom. Her sister came back to the house, and I marveled at the fact that this woman had grown up with my mother. The stories she told were full of adventure and love. It ended up being a magical party, full of love and honor to my mother.

Later that evening, Troy pulled me out of my body and we both went and pulled my father out of his body. As we arrived at my mother's home on the astral level, my father could not believe his eyes. Mom opened the door and gave my dad a welcome smile and a hug. It was such a sweet reunion, my eyes filled with tears. They hugged for a very long time and then all of us went inside. Dad just would not let go of Mom. It was as if he never wanted her to leave him again.

Once all of us were inside, Mom stood up, and tried to explain to my dad and I, just what it was like for her to die.

She began by saying, "My mom and Troy were at my bedside continuously throughout the last few weeks of my life. When I saw my mom by my bedside, I knew that I would soon be joining her." She looked at my father, and said, "While I was very unhappy about leaving you behind, I had become extremely tired of my pain-ridden body."

"Mom," I said, "did you have to die on your birthday? Was that necessary?"

Mom paused for a moment, and then said, "I wanted to leave after my birthday. But I was in a great deal of pain, and I just could not hold on any longer. I was trying to hold-on until after all of you had celebrated my birthday with me and had gone home. I knew how important all of you felt that day was, and that you had already guessed that it would be my last earthly birthday. However, as the pain became more and more intense, I just wanted to leave, and began calling for my own mother to come and take me home. I saw my mom first and then I saw Troy. I asked them if it was time for me to go. They nodded their heads yes, and began to pull me out of my body, via the top of my head."

As she paused, I interrupted her by saying, "When I visited you in the hospital, each time I would lightly touch you, to ascertain what area you were going to use to leave your body. I had assumed that it would be via your heart area because people who have led better than average lives often leave through that area. I knew you had led, what to me was, a good life. Imagine my surprise when I felt the top of your head and realized that it was very hot; you were going to leave by the top of your head. No other area showed any activity related to you leaving your body. I had been right. I was amazed."

"May I continue?" My mother asked.

"Oh, sorry Mom. Please do."

She continued by saying, "As I began to leave my body, I felt areas of my body growing cold. It was really a weird feeling. But, the lightness I was feeling outweighed my curiosity. Once I was out of my body, I suddenly felt so free that I just wanted to dance and sing. My mother and Troy grabbed my arms and asked me if I could see the light. I turned around and, for a moment, got a glimpse of my body lying on the bed so still and cold. There was no cord that I could see connecting me to my body. I knew then that I would never again reside in that body. As I turned around, I could see the light that Troy had inquired about, shining brightly ahead in the distance. As I got closer to it I could see the tunnel, just as you had described it to me for so many years, Kathie. It seemed to pulsate and glow with an unearthly light."

Mom paused for a moment and turned away from us. When she turned around, there were tears in her eyes. She looked at me and my father.

"There were so many people in the tunnel, some of whom I had not seen for many a year. They all surrounded me and gave such hugs that I knew I was indeed coming home."

"Remember Jo?" she asked me.

"Of course I do. You and she were the best of friends throughout most of your adult life."

My mom smiled and said, "She was in the tunnel. Our reunion was so sweet. We immediately began talking with each other as if no time had passed. All around me I could see other such reunions taking place within the tunnel of light. I saw other family members later after I had actually arrived. The tunnel is usually reserved for immediate family or friends."

Mom looked at my dad and said, "It was so sweet and joyful, Manning. You don't have to worry about not seeing me again. I will come for you at the time of your passing and will make sure that your mom is in the tunnel with us."

Oh happy day, I thought. She was happy and comfortable. Even though I would no longer be able to talk to her in her earthly body, I now knew that she was happy here with her loved ones.

My dad was silent for a long time. Perhaps, he was reflecting on all that she had said. Because after a while he finally spoke to my mom.

"Honey, I will miss you and think about you every day until we can be together again."

Mom smiled, and gave dad the most loving hug and kiss I had ever seen between the two of them.

"I will be waiting for you. Just call me whenever you want to see me and I will come and get you later that night. We will be able to visit during the time that your body is asleep," she said.

Dad smiled. Not even death would keep him from his beloved wife.

Mom then turned to me and said, "Kathie, I know how much you will miss me for what will seem like a very long time. It will be a while before I come and get you out of your body for your last time. But just know that I will love you forever and I will be smiling at you from here with much love and peace. You will be able to come and visit me any time you want to."

I stared at her face for a long time. She was so happy. Her life here on the astral realm suited her.

All too soon, it was time for us to leave. The love and peace that surrounded us was truly amazing.

As we traveled back through the tunnel, I could see all of the reunions that were taking place. There were so many happy shouts from both sides of the tunnel. As I thought about what I was seeing around me, I was reminded of the many classes I had attended on the heavenly levels. There is purpose to living an earthly life. We can learn from life itself.

Troy dropped my dad off first at the home he had shared with my mom. As I turned to wave goodbye, I noticed with great joy that Mom was sitting next to Dad and holding his hand. She smiled at me and indicated that she would be staying with my dad for a little bit, just to help him adjust to his new life. I blew a kiss to her and then I was once again in my own bed.

I thought about what my mom had described to my dad and I. Death does not need to hold any fear for people. It is just a matter of getting out of your body for the last time. Then, in that beautiful tunnel of light, you will once again be reunited with your loved ones. My mom is now happier than I have ever seen her; some day, I know she will return for me. What a glorious reunion that will be!

For more information about the author as well as a schedule of seminars and events where she is scheduled to speak, please visit www.KathieJordan.com